PINOCHET
The Politics of Torture
HUGH O'SHAUGHNESSY

To James
with great
thanks to
your ecosystem

Hugo

LATIN
AMERICA
BUREAU

LAB

The right of Hugh O'Shaughnessy to be identified as the author of this work has been asserted by him in accordance with the Copyright, Designs and Patents Act 1988

First published in the UK in 2000 by:

Latin America Bureau (Research and Action) Ltd
1 Amwell Street, London EC1R 1UL

A CIP catalogue record is available from the British Library

ISBN: 1 899365 41 9

First published in the USA in 2000 by:

New York University Press
New York, NY 10003

Cover photographs: *La Nación*
Cover design: Andy Dark
Printed and bound: Russell Press, Nottingham

To my parents, Charles Hilary and Mary,
with love and gratitude

Requiescant a laboribus suis, opera enim illorum sequuntur illos

Permissions

Diary of a Chilean Concentration Camp, by Hernán Valdés, published by Victor Gollancz, 1975. Reprinted by permission of David Higham Associates. © 1975 by Hernán Valdés.

Extract from *Audacity to Believe*, by Sheila Cassidy is reprinted here by permission of the author.

Acknowledgements

The task of writing this book has been made easier by the willing support I have received from many friends and colleagues. I received my first encouragement from my colleagues on the council of management and the staff of the Latin America Bureau, LAB, with which I have been associated with since its foundation in London in 1977. Valuable other help and encouragement came in Britain from Dick Barber-Might, Geoffrey Bindman, Professor James Dunkerley, Dr James Ferguson, Mike Gatehouse, the staff of the Medical Foundation for the Care of Victims of Torture, Paul Lashmar, Alex Morrowsmith, James Murphy, Dr Robinson Rojas, Jorge Silva, Diane Dixon and Frances Webber and in Chile from Ruth Bradley, General Luis Cortés Villa, Armen Kouyoumdjian, Senator Hernán Larrain, Hernán Millas, Hernán Montealegre and his wife Raquel, Herman and Adriana Schwember, Raúl Sohr and his wife Imogen, Armando Uribe, Mario Valenzuela and his wife Milka, Raúl Vergara and Pepe Zalaquett. In Spain Juan Garcés and Elizabeth Nash offered valuable assistance while in Uruguay I was helped by Samuel Blixen, Senator Rafael Michelini and his brother Deputy Felipe Michelini. In Argentina and Brazil Horacio Verbitsky and Bernardo Kuchinsky respectively have been brave and constant foes of the many dictators in the Southern Cone of South America who were united with Pinochet in the Condor operation. In Paraguay I benefited from excellent work on Operation Condor by many including Dr Alfredo Boccia Paz and Rosa María Ortiz.

I have made much use of Pinochet's own memoirs. (The effort of ploughing through page upon page of material where women are 'lady wives' or 'lady mothers', where the author's friends among the military are 'brave, frank and good soldiers' and where almost all civilian politicians are reprehensible was a taxing one. That acute observer and wordsmith Armando Uribe has called the general's style *siútico-militar* – what in Britain would be known as Pooterish – sentimental or coyly dainty.)

My special thanks go to Jean McNeil, my editor at LAB.

My wife Georgie has been a constant help, not least for the supreme dislike she still harbours for the ugly side of Chilean society which she observed during the time our family spent in Chile in the 1960s.

Hugh O'Shaughnessy

Contents

1

The Arrest

'The Chileans will tell you with pride they are often
called the English of South America.'
Augusto Pinochet interviewed by John Lee Anderson,
The New Yorker, September 1998.

Honoured guest

'As soon as they've operated on me, I'm off.'
Augusto Pinochet, London, 1 October 1998.

On 21 September 1998 General Augusto Pinochet Ugarte, lately
dictator of the Republic of Chile, arrived at Heathrow Airport.
Pinochet was travelling on a Chilean diplomatic passport as a former
head of state, now Life Senator. The red-carpet reception at the
airport's VIP suite, whose use was paid for by the Foreign and
Commonwealth Office, was discreet but becoming of a foreign
former president. He was spared the indignity of explaining himself
to an immigration officer or having to present his luggage to customs
officials.

The Independent newspaper reported the presence of Pinochet in
Britain, but it was hardly big news. The General had been to Britain
several times since 1990, when he had reverted from being president
to merely commander-in-chief of the Chilean army. As an important
arms purchaser he had been a welcome guest not just of British
Aerospace, Europe's largest arms manufacturer, but also of the
Conservative governments. He had also visited Britain after the
Labour Party came to power in Britain in May 1997 and, while he
may not have been welcomed with open arms, there was no bar to
the entry to Britain of a man who a quarter of a century before had
been a principal hate figure of the Labour Party.

Over the next few days Pinochet's activities were consistent with previous trips to London: he met Lady Thatcher, former prime minister, for tea. He went shopping – he was known to favour Harrods and Fortnum and Mason's – and gave an interview to *The New Yorker* magazine in which he told his interviewer, John Lee Anderson, a biographer of Che Guevara, that 'my history teacher always told me that the lives of dictators end badly.'

Were it not for the presence of his bodyguards, Pinochet could probably pass incognito in any situation in busy London. He does not fit the stereotype of a dictator. He is of shorter than average stature. Like Fidel Castro, he has a high voice, which he often uses in a rasping way, perhaps to disguise its register. It is true that in the years after the 1973 military coup his image put him well within the moustache-and sunglasses brigade of South American dictators. (Indeed he had a lifelong penchant for wearing dark glasses.) He also maintained a well-clipped moustache and he retained more hair than many men of his age. But now, at 82 years old, he wore conservative suits instead of the military uniform he was constantly pictured in during his regime, and his hair had turned to a respectable silver.

In the course of his visit he took medical advice about a herniated disc in his spinal column and at the beginning of October he was admitted to a private London hospital, the London Clinic. There then took place a delicate operation on a man of 82 who suffered from diabetes and who wore a heart pacemaker. Should anything have gone wrong with the procedure there was a danger that his spinal cord could have been damaged, with the subsequent risk of paraplegia or the loss of the use of his lower limbs. He would normally have been expected to remain prone in a hospital bed for some weeks while his backbone recovered. He would then return directly home to Santiago, the capital of Chile. But events were soon to take an unprecedented turn.

In the late evening of Friday 16 October 1998 two plainclothes officers of the Metropolitan Police, the force which polices London, entered Pinochet's private hospital room, where the former dictator lay sleeping. The officers woke him and proceeded to state that they were acting in response to a Red Notice warrant issued by Interpol on behalf of the Spanish authorities, and that they were placing him under arrest on charges of the murder and torture of Spanish citizens. (There is some evidence that the Chilean authorities knew of the move in advance, but they were in no position to move Pinochet precipitately out of the United Kingdom for fear of rendering him a paraplegic.)

The General was still under post-operative medication and in a confused haze. While his English is poor, he seemed to understand what was happening to him. Armed policemen were posted at his room and at the entrances to the Clinic and the General's own bodyguards were disarmed.

Just after mid-day the next day, 17 October, the Home Office, Britain's interior ministry, announced the arrest to the world.

The reaction from victims of the General's regime was immediate and euphoric. Dr Oscar Soto, the former personal doctor of Salvador Allende, the democratically-elected President of Chile deposed by Pinochet's coup d'état of 11 September 1973, speaking to *The Guardian*, said: 'It is a great triumph of justice. Pinochet must now give account for more than 3,000 deaths, exiles and tortures in the 17 years of his dictatorship.' Newspapers in the United Kingdom and around the world carried articles written by individual Chileans exiled by the General's regime, who spoke of their relief and feelings of vindication. Many said how the General's sudden arrest was like having a memory box pried open after twenty-five years, to find inside the hurt and terror inspired by the events of September 1973 surprisingly intact.

As for Pinochet, if he were inclined to whimsical associations, the place of his arrest might have struck the General as particularly ironic. There had been a Clínica Londres, or London Clinic, in the Calle Almirante Barroso in Santiago. It was used by his secret police to care for their victims who had been particularly damaged by torture. In that London Clinic people were nursed back to health so as to be able to withstand further bouts of torture, and eventually, in many cases, to die.

The nature of Pinochet's internment, the arrest of a former head of state travelling on a diplomatic passport, made it the first of its kind in Britain or in Europe. More importantly, it was an unprecedented use of international law. Prompted by the determination of one Spanish investigating judge, Pinochet's arrest immediately established a milestone in international legal practice. A former head of state of one country (Chile) had been arrested on a warrant from a judge of another (Spain), and seized in a third territory (Britain). Under the international agreements which govern Interpol, an Interpol warrant prepared in due form virtually obliged the British Government to take action or provide good reason why it would not.

Almost immediately, Conservative politicians expressed their outrage at the arrest, Lady Thatcher leading the outcry. Chile, Lady Thatcher said, had been 'a good friend to Britain', giving it invaluable help in its war with Argentina over the Falklands in 1982. Pinochet had quietly authorised the Royal Air Force to have landing rights at a number of Chilean airfields during the conflict. British troops operated from Chilean territory in Tierra del Fuego and the intelligence given to the British from the Chilean radars – which in any event constantly monitor Argentine air force bases – was a great asset. It was even said by some military men that the largest single loss of British troops, when Argentine air force Mirages and Skyhawks raided Bluff Cove on 8 June 1982, had been due to the fact that Chilean radar coverage had momentarily faltered.

Certainly Pinochet genuinely liked and admired Britain. He had often remarked how he liked the civility to be found in London and the Englishman's determination to play by the rules. I myself had written about one previous visit where he had been delighted to be able to buy ties for himself at Harrods and eat in good restaurants.

But few people were aware of the ex-dictator in their midst. After the arrest, apart from ecstatic Chile solidarity groups on the one hand, and the vehement response emanating from Lady Thatcher and members of her ex-government on the other, most people simply wondered what the furore was about.

By now, twenty-five years after the coup, millions of British people were hardly old enough to have had much of a grasp of the events which led to Pinochet's seizing of power in Chile on Tuesday, 11 September 1973. Of the older generation, some may have remembered the Labour Party's active hostility to the Chilean dictatorship. Others may have recalled the important dockers' unions boycott of Chilean cargoes at British ports, notably Liverpool. Others may recall the pickets which stopped the engines of the Hawker Hunter aircraft, the type which had been used to bomb Allende's presidential palace, being returned to the Chilean air force from the Rolls-Royce plant in the Scottish town of East Kilbride where they had been reconditioned. A few may dimly remember the unwillingness of right-thinking members of the middle class to consume Chilean wine and fruit.

From Britain's Labour Government there was little public response to the arrest. Those who commented on the case stressed that it was a judicial, not a political, decision, and that the General had been arrested through a legally valid process. Government members made little comment and deferred to the man ultimately charged with responding to the Pinochet case, Jack Straw, the Home Secretary.

For Chile, however, and for Augusto Pinochet Ugarte personally, his arrest had an immediate effect. It punctured the military and political image of a man who was, and remains, for better or for worse, remarkable.

During and after his seventeen-year reign as dictator of Chile, this son of a lower middle-class family had seized supreme power for himself in a country of more than 12 million people, and struck terror into the hearts of his enemies at home and abroad. He had moulded his own country in a way few, if any, had done before him. He has also been directly, personally responsible for some of the worst human rights abuses in the post-war era. Like the majority of his comrades-in-arms he eluded justice until that October night when he awoke to find policemen at his London bedside.

The man himself, the fear and power he has commanded, and the events of his life combine to tell a powerful story of betrayal and treachery, of opportunism and ambition. But who is this man, Augusto Pinochet? Where did he come from, and how did he end up as the central figure in the most complex case in international law of the late twentieth century?

Two days before his detention *The Guardian* had asked me to write a polemic drawing attention to Pinochet's presence in London. The piece, which called for his arrest, was printed in that newspaper on 15 October 1998 under a suitably incendiary title. I composed this article on Wednesday, two days before he was arrested. It was written somewhat tongue in cheek, and I had no expectation whatsoever that the course I advocated would be adopted within hours.

'A murderer among us'

We are on the edge of a marvellous international coup, which will not only hit at crime here in Britain but also strike fear into terrorists worldwide. It will, too, send a strong signal that Robin Cook, the Foreign Secretary, is serious about his ethical foreign policy and that Tony Blair's government is keen to do all it can to uphold the rule of international law.

There is a foreign terrorist in our midst who is hiding somewhere in London. He is responsible for the savage torture of a British surgeon. He is also a murderer. In a calculated insult to the United States Government he did what the Iranians, the Iraqis and the Libyans have never dared to do. He sent his assassins to the heart of the diplomatic quarter in Washington where they killed one of his opponents, a former diplomat, by blowing up his car, and he encompassed the death of thousands of his own countrymen. He called for the president of his country to be stripped and thrown to his death from an aircraft and the other day I heard a recording of him giving an order to that effect.

The facts of his culpability are clear, indeed uncontested. He has often boasted about them. There is a warrant out for his arrest and Britain is under an international obligation under the terms of Article 6 of the UN Convention Against Torture and Other Cruel, Inhuman and Degrading Treatment or Punishment to detain him and send him for trial.

He has murky business dealings with well-known British firms and his name is well-known to the Department of Trade and the Export Credits Guarantee Department. Sadly, through police negligence which must be attributed to Jack Straw's predecessors at the Home Office, he slipped through the net on previous visits to this country. He boasts that he buys his ties at Harrods and shops in Fortnum and Mason. But he is slippery. He has made various visits to well-guarded government establishments, (the National Army Museum is one such), but no one from the Met's Anti-Terrorist Squad or the Ministry of Defence's own highly skilled police has yet felt his collar.

The nearest he came to danger was on one of his previous trips to London when a waiter at the River Café at Hammersmith recognised him. He was sitting in a corner facing the door with his goons, doubtless desperate men, guarding the entrance. These fellow terrorists of his are known to go around armed. If they were on this occasion – and from my knowledge of him I am pretty sure that this would have been the case – he would have been insulting the British Government as he had already insulted the US Government. It is inconceivable that a British minister or official in his right mind would have knowingly allowed a terrorist hit squad to swan round this capital with lethal weapons.

Lady Rogers, owner of the café, told me she had to think fast. In a flash before he moved off, she wisely decided to take what he paid for the bill and send it to Amnesty International. But tragically the Anti-Terrorist Squad was nowhere in sight.

If this man escapes from Britain once again, a great many people here and abroad will want to know why. Irresponsible commentators will cast doubt on the idea of an ethical foreign policy, the Home Secretary will be under something of a cloud and the already difficult position of Sir Paul Condon as Commissioner of the Metropolitan Police will finally become untenable.

But possibly he may not get away this time. Keep your eyes peeled, particularly if you are shopping in the West End or visiting the National Army Museum today. If you are a patient in the London Clinic be particularly alert. Some people say he's holed up there for treatment.

I shall be listening to the radio and television news today, waiting hopefully for the arrest of the former dictator of Chile, General Augusto Pinochet Ugarte.

The Guardian, 15 October 1998

II

The Making of a General

A sensitive boy

'My maternal grandmother thought that her first grandchild had to be a child prodigy and wanted me to learn to read before I was four and so she sent me to an infants' school.'
Augusto Pinochet, *Camino Recorrido*

The future dictator was born in Valparaiso on 25 November 1915, the eldest of three boys and three girls. His father Augusto was apparently the descendant of one Guillaume Pinochet, a Frenchman who arrived in Chile in the early 18th century. Augusto senior worked as a customs agent in a British-owned trading company, Williamson Balfour, in Valparaiso, Chile's main port. His mother Avelina Ugarte was a pious housewife with little formal education but an enormously strong will.

Since Spanish colonists had settled there in the sixteenth century, Valparaiso, the 'Valley of Paradise', had been the gateway to the Central Valley of Chile, the fertile heart of the country with a climate similar to that of California. During the four centuries that Spain ruled Chile as its colony, the narrow strip of land was not the most favoured part of the King of Spain's dominions. Unlike Peru or Mexico, it contained few precious metals. Its use, if it had any, was as a source of food and other supplies for the imperial city of Lima, where the Viceroy held his court amid great pomp.

The full name given to Chile's new capital by Spain was Santiago del Nuevo Extremo – Santiago in the Wild South. The models of the city in the Museum of Santiago today show a very un-prepossessing settlement with few buildings of architectural merit. Had there been many put up they would anyway in all likelihood have been shaken down by the frequent earthquakes and tremors which characterise the region. In contrast to the colonial splendours of Rio de Janeiro or Mexico City Chilean cities can boast only of squat churches and palaces with mud walls thick enough to survive these frequent shakings.

About a hundred kilometres to the west of Santiago, Valparaiso was built in a vast natural amphitheatre around a sheltered harbour three miles across. Since Chile had achieved its independence from Spain in 1817, and thereby the freedom to trade with any nation, the port had prospered. There was a large colony of foreigners, many of them British, as Britain was by far Chile's most important trading partner. The Valley of Paradise was the first big Pacific port for ships sailing between the Atlantic and the Pacific around the Straits of Magellan at the tip of South America, which before the construction of the Panama Canal in 1914 was the only sea route between the two oceans.

But by the year of Pinochet's birth Valparaiso was experiencing a crisis of which his father, who worked in the customs house, would have been painfully aware. The Panama Canal had opened the previous year and the world's seafarers were beginning to adjust to the new, much shorter and more convenient route.

In addition the more southerly port of Concepción, where a coal industry had been established, had long been poaching Valparaiso's trade in bunkering ocean-going vessels. Valparaiso's city fathers were doing their best to keep their city competitive by building vast new moorings capable of taking the world's largest ships. They also moved to clear up rapidly after the frequent earthquakes which levelled Valparaiso even more frequently than other Chilean towns. Despite these efforts, trade withered, particularly during the Great Depression, and brought hardship to those like Pinochet's father whose livelihood depended on buoyant trade.

According to Pinochet's cousin Mónica Madariaga – whom he was later to appoint minister of justice – Augusto, or 'Tito' as he was known, was by the age of two a child with a mind of his own. His mother used to like dressing him in a sailor suit and forbade him to eat ice cream lest the suit be stained. He rolled round on the floor to get it dirty anyway. Pinochet himself recounts how one day when he was very young she went chasing him with a broom in the garden when he was suddenly stung by a bee and let out a scream. Avelina stopped, comforted the boy, and then seized the broom and gave him the clout she had been intending. A short time before she died she confessed she had always thought that her Augusto would become president 'but I didn't tell anyone so that they wouldn't laugh at me'.

According to his own account, Augusto Pinochet was a sensitive child. At a young age he was taken to his first cinema to see a silent film. It showed a gun fight and, as the pianist banged out a dramatic accompaniment, the little boy screamed. The next scene involved a railway train rushing towards the audience and Tito tried to hide under the seat, bellowing in such panic that the lights had to be turned on while his mother took him out. 'The only thing I wanted,' he remarked, 'was to escape from that torture chamber.'

Otherwise he played happily enough in the streets and squares of the city. Perhaps his first inspiration to become a soldier came from hearing the music of the military and naval bands in Valparaiso's parks or watching the construction of the monument to the heroes of the battle of Iquique of 1879 during the War of the Pacific. His sister Nena recalls that he passed his time playing with his drums and trumpets. The young Augusto had been always proud of his French connection and later developed a great admiration for Louis XIV and Napoleon. In particular he was moved by the tales of Francisco Valette, the husband of his maternal grandmother. Valette went off during the First World War to help defend France from the Germans, was wounded in battle and returned to Valparaiso in 1921.

When he was five or six and already dreaming of becoming a soldier he damaged his left knee in a road accident. Later a local doctor was keen to amputate. Avelina prayed to Our Lady of Perpetual Succour for a cure, promising that she would dress in coffee coloured material for fifteen years if he recovered and that he would do the same for ten years, or two years if he indeed became a soldier. A visiting German doctor disagreed with the local diagnosis and prescribed sunlight. The swollen knee was cured in weeks. The vow, Pinochet recounts in his memoirs, was kept by mother and son. The devout Pinochet was later to fix in a local church an ex voto plaque to the Virgin bearing the words:

Thank you, Mother mine
Succour me always
Ensign A.Pinochet
1936

Augusto's school days began when parents sent him to school first in the San Rafael Seminary, where he was expelled for naughtiness, then to an establishment run by the Marist Brothers at Quillota, a pleasant inland town famed for its orchards. He ended his boyhood education at the French-run College of the Sacred Hearts in Valparaiso. Rafael Agustín Gumucio, a prominent politician whose brother had been a classmate of the future dictator, recalled that the college was full of the sons of richer families than Pinochet's. 'Think of the difficulties he must have had to fit in,' Gumucio reflected.

In none of his schools did Pinochet show academic aptitude. He achieved marks of no more than 3 (on a grade from 1 to 7) for seven of the eight tests he underwent in 1929. But his education in the best Catholic schools in the neighbourhood and his mother's piety – she took the family to mass every Sunday – did give him an appreciation of the importance of the Catholic Church.

Knowledge of religion was to come in useful in his later political career, when he had to sort out his Catholic friends and sympathisers, many of whom were to be found in the Vatican, from the many opponents who stood up to him within Chile's own powerful Catholic Church. Though he later became a freemason early in his career and thus flouted Catholic teaching, he was always careful to try and project an image of piety by frequently taking the sacraments and publicising his devotion to the Virgin of Mount Carmel, protectress of the Chilean army.

One woman who knew Pinochet well and who is quoted by Pablo Azócar in his book *Pinochet: Epitáfio para un Tirano* (*Pinochet: Epitaph for a Tyrant*) said that his mother Avelina was a person of great astuteness though she had not had much education. 'She was very energetic and very, very authoritarian. If she had told him to go and live at the North Pole, Augusto would have gone. She was his lighthouse, his compass, the finger which pointed out his way to him. She was fixated on military life and Augusto as a result was a soldier. He couldn't have ever contradicted her.'

In uniform at last

'The things that interested me most were classes in tactics,
strategy and military history.'
Augusto Pinochet, *Camino Recorrido*

The Chilean armed forces did not draw its men from the highest ranks of Chilean society. The most 'aristocratic' arm was the navy, which was closely linked to the British and which looked back to Lord Cochrane, the Scottish nobleman who had been its founder. Most wealthy Chileans were from the old-established families whose wealth tended to come from land and would not have considered putting their sons down for the army. With a few exceptions, Chilean army officers were drawn more from the modest middle-class such as Pinochet's own family.

Pinochet entered the army in 1933 as an officer cadet. It was his third attempt. By the time Pinochet came to its lower ranks, the Chilean army had earned itself a good reputation. It had never lost a war. Not for nothing was the national motto '*Por la Razón o La Fuerza*', 'By Reason or Force'. Certainly at the beginning of the nineteenth century Chilean soldiers had fought well for their independence from Spain under Bernardo O'Higgins, the illegitimate son of Ambrosio O'Higgins, the adventurer who had emigrated from Ireland to join the service of the King of Spain and had risen to the rank of Viceroy of Peru.

By 1836 Chile had begun the first of two wars against Peru. In the second, the War of the Pacific, the Chileans carried all before them against an alliance of Peru and Bolivia. In 1879 they occupied the then-Bolivian port of Antofagasta for good and cut Bolivia's tenuous links with the Pacific. By January 1881 they were back again in occupation of the Peruvian capital.

Despite their bravery and élan, the Chilean infantry were, it was said, no more than 'peasants with rifles' who won more because they were more numerous than because they were better trained and equipped. Soon, however, German-sponsored training was to change all that.

In 1885, after the Franco-Prussian War had established Prussia as a first-class military power in Europe, a Chilean mission was clever enough to tempt a remarkable young officer into Chile's service.

13

Captain Emil Koerner had had a good war, fighting at Woerth, Sedan and Bazeilles, actions which led to the occupation of Paris by the triumphant Prussians. He caught the eye of a General Moltke, who gave him confidential missions in France, Italy, Spain and Russia. Koerner then went on to staff college, graduating third in a class whose top student was Hindenburg, a man destined to become a powerful figure in the First World War and president of Germany thereafter.

By 1885 Koerner was professor of military history, tactics and ballistics in the artillery school at Charlottenburg. That year he signed a five-year contract, automatically renewable, with the Chileans. With a handful of compatriots Koerner started an Academy of War in Santiago and had the good fortune to be on hand in 1891 when civil war broke out between the energetic President José Manuel Balmaceda and the conservative Congress, which Koerner supported. After the defeat and suicide of Balmaceda, Koerner wrote back triumphantly to Kaiser Wilhelm in Berlin of the superiority of 'great old Prussian traditions on the far shores of the Pacific Ocean.'

By the end of the 19th century Chile was the paramount power on the Pacific coast of South America. Germans stayed in Chile to train the army until 1930, well after the Treaty of Versailles which sought to reduce Germany's military power for ever. The German trainers' job was made all the easier by the receptiveness of the many Chilean army officers who went to visit and train in Germany. The young Pinochet, as a teenager aspiring to a military career, would certainly have realised the role of the Germans and seen their mark in the field-grey uniforms of the army, the infantry drill, its goose-step and the military bands with their tubas, euphoniums and glockenspiels, all of which are still part of the Chilean army to this day.

The cadet would also have appreciated the very real educative process the army was exerting on its recruits. Koerner had reported with pride that under his command 80 per cent of illiterate recruits could read and write within a month of joining the army where they were also taught the elements of hygiene, temperance – Pinochet himself would be a life-long non-drinker – and respect for due authority.

At the Academy of War officers were given a thorough grounding in their profession, based on a scrupulous study of Europe's wars and the teaching of German as the first foreign language, which elicited protests from France and the United States.

The idea that the armed forces in Chile were 'apolitical' dates from the time of Koerner's influence and from the actions of the military in the 1891 civil war. This myth of the non-partisan nature of Chile's armed forces, which was well embroidered by middle-class civilian politicians and had currency up to 1973 and even beyond, was not the exclusive creation of the conservative middle-class. As the country moved into a period of social change even the left repeated it, with increasing desperation as the events leading up to 1973 will show.

Certainly Chile avoided the constant military coups which made the politics of many Latin American countries, notably Bolivia, Argentina and El Salvador, a laughing stock. But in 1811, as a sense of Chilean nationhood began to be born, there was one failed military coup against the civilian government and two successful ones, both the work of a soldier, José Miguel Carrera. Time and again there were threats to civilian governments from headstrong officers.

The year before Pinochet entered the army was the end of an unusual period of comic opera military politics in Chile. In 1927 a ambitious soldier who had served a rather nerveless civilian president as minister of war decided he wanted the presidency for himself. General Carlos Ibáñez del Campo held an election where he contrived to be the only candidate and to win 80 per cent of the votes. Thereafter he achieved many things but ruled with an iron rod until he was forced from office in 1931 as Chile wrestled with the Great Depression. There followed a period of chaos culminating in the establishment in 1932 of a Socialist Republic under Marmaduke Grove, a colonel in the air force, which lasted all of twelve days.

As the young Augusto started his career the country was beginning to settle down again under an able elected civilian president, Arturo Alessandri. Still, there was anti-military sentiment in the air and the cadets were told not to go into the city in uniform lest they be heckled.

In 1937, at age twenty-two, the cadet emerged as an ensign in the infantry and was posted to the School of Infantry at San Bernardo. In September of that year Pinochet's regimental life started when he was sent south to Concepción to join the Chacabuco Regiment. He called Concepción, in the green and wooded country south of Santiago, 'a wonderland'. It was the ideal place for Pinochet to ponder his country's naval successes, as in the nearby naval base of Talcahuano sat one of the greatest prizes Chile had ever captured in war: the warship Huáscar, once the pride of the Peruvian navy and named after one of the last of the Inca imperial family.

During the War of the Pacific this squat, ironclad vessel armed with two powerful guns amidships had for a time instilled fear in the Chilean navy. In May 1879 the Peruvians dispatched her to lift the Chilean blockade of Iquique, a port vital for Peru's nitrate exports. Against her the Chileans could muster only the sailing ships Covadonga and Esmeralda, commanded by Captain Arturo Prat. The Huáscar destroyed the Esmeralda but Prat, his men following, managed to board the Peruvian vessel and was killed on her metal deck. Chile took its revenge later that year when the Huáscar was captured at the battle of Angamos and later towed south, where the Chileans kept it as a trophy of the conflict.

In 1938 the political scene changed again. The Popular Front government of President Pedro Aguirre Cerda, which grouped Socialists and Communists, was freely voted into power. It was the most interesting political development in Chile in several decades, but according to the memoirs he published in 1990, Pinochet and his young fellow officers were bored with politics and doubtful of the good faith of those who devoted their lives to it.

A few weeks before the Socialists came to power in October 1938, the National Socialist Movement, a Chilean group which modelled themselves on Adolf Hitler's National Socialist Party, attempted a putsch in Santiago, seizing a number of offices. Forces loyal to the government stormed their stronghold and during the siege a carabinero, or armed policeman, was killed. The police took terrible revenge on the men they captured, killing 58 of them as well as three innocent civilians. This event impressed Pinochet's circle of friends and, he adds in his memoirs, made them distrust foreign ideologies all the more.

16

In 1939, Pinochet was back in his native city of Valparaiso as second lieutenant in the Maipo Regiment. This was the healthy outdoor life he had always wanted, with many companions and good, clean fun, including practical jokes.

In his memoirs he tells of how the captain in command of his unit on a field day on horseback, a man given to practical jokes, gave the order that everyone should go and buy eggs for the officers' mess. The fresh eggs were stuffed in the soldiers' capes but on return to barracks the order came to dismount and parade immediately. The young Pinochet gave his cape to his batman and formed up the men for inspection by the major. The latter, seeing the bulging capes, went round whacking every one with the result that each soldier ended up standing in a pool of yolk and egg whites, to the captain's great mirth.

Such amusing antics aside, from his early days as a soldier Pinochet demonstrated an interest in study. In the 1940s he pursued all the opportunities for learning that the forces offered him, specialising in geopolitics and military geography – subjects particularly relevant to the armed forces of a country as long, thin, apparently indefensible and as surrounded by disgruntled neighbours as is Chile.

During this time he also met the woman who was to be his wife. The twenty-seven year-old Pinochet met Lucía Hiriart, the daughter of politician Osvaldo Hiriart, when she was a fifteen-year old schoolgirl at the Liceo San Bernardo situated opposite the officers' mess.

She and a friend were collecting money for charity when her friend's father appeared with a young infantry officer. The father put five pesos in the collecting box and both men took flags for their buttonholes. Later, after they were married, Augusto told Lucía he had taken a flag without putting money in the box because he had no money on him at all. According to Pablo Azócar, one of Pinochet's biographers, at the end of the 1930s the family had so little money that the young officer had to take six months leave from the army to work with his father at a job which would give the family more money than he was earning as a second lieutenant. (Even today a second lieutenant in the Chilean army today earns the equivalent of only £2,640 per annum.)

At the time he met her Lucía was the girlfriend of an air force cadet. But Tito, twelve years her senior, pursued the fifteen year-old, winning the nickname of 'Infanticida' ('Babykiller') from his comrades. Augusto and Lucía were married on 30 January 1942. The wedding photograph published in his memoirs shows the fine upstanding infantry officer in his white tunic, his moustache trimmed and his sword by his side. He is carrying his helmet with a white plume on his left arm while his bride puts her white-gloved hand on his right arm. Both wear expressions of determination and resoluteness.

With his marriage Pinochet was moving out of the orbit of his mother who had so powerfully formed him into that of another woman who was to shape him with even more application and tenacity.

His new wife's family would also influence him. Osvaldo, Pinochet's father-in-law, was chubby-cheeked and affable. He belonged to the Radical Party, which was identified with the lower middle class, civil servants and a certain Masonic anti-clericalism. Hiriart was later to become minister of the interior and sponsored Pinochet to become a freemason. However, Pinochet seems never to have played an active role in the masonic craft. One version has it that he was struck off the role of masons in Valparaiso because of his general apathy and lack of participation in the movement. Nevertheless, mason or non-mason, he was to make much use of his masonic father-in-law's powerful connections over the years.

For her part, his mother-in-law seems to have felt her daughter could have done better for herself than a young officer who hadn't had money to put in a collecting box for charity.

In 1943 the couple's first daughter Inés Lucía was born, soon to be followed by Augusto Osvaldo, María Verónica, Marco Antonió and Jacqueline Marie, the latter named after John Kennedy's wife.

As the Pinochet family increased, far to the north the war hurtled on. In Chile, as in the rest of Latin America, the Second World War was not a matter of great consequence, except that it offered great opportunities for making money by selling precious raw materials to the Allies. As the Second World War developed, Britain and the US presented Santiago with much evidence of the activities of Nazi espionage among the numerous German colonies in Chile. In Chile, as throughout Latin America, the allies were worried lest Nazism strike deeper roots than it already had, and that Nazi Germany find in the region the raw materials that it needed for its war machine.

For more than a century Chile had opened its doors to immigrants from Germany and given them grants of land at the southern end of the Central Valley. In parts of southern Chile to this day it is not unknown for an obvious foreigner to be hailed with the greeting, '*Sprechen Sie Deutsch?*' Pinochet's father meanwhile had been put on an Allied blacklist for having commercial relations with citizens of the Axis powers.

The Chilean government did not break relations with Germany, Italy and Japan until January 1943. War was never formally declared against Hitler, though in February 1945 President Juan Antonio Ríos acknowledged one existed with Japan. Chile had taken action just in time to allow it to take part in the foundation of the United Nations.

Up the ladder

'When we disembarked at Iquique we found we had nowhere to go.'
Augusto Pinochet, *Camino Recorrido*

As the war ended Pinochet, now a captain, was transferred with his family to the Carampangue regiment in Iquique, a town in the far north of the country on the edge of the Atacama Desert.

The Atacama, a wilderness of ochre rocks and sand dunes and bare mountains, is devoid of rain, intolerably hot by day, and often intolerably cold by night. The only green is found in the rare oases filled with palm trees and in the occasional streams fed from the High Andes.

The Atacama is also one of the most extensive salt flats in the continent, and is criss-crossed with seams of minerals from copper to lithium. This was the reason the Chileans had invaded and captured the area from Peru and Bolivia in the 19th century – certainly it was not for its architectural and natural charms.

Since the beginning of the 19th century the nitrates of the Atacama were to be found in almost all the world's agricultural fertilisers. Nitrate created enormous fortunes for the nitrate mine owners, but after the invention of synthetic fertilisers in Germany at the beginning of the 20th century the mining towns turned to ghost towns, and Humberstone, Santa Laura, Peña Chica, Guanilla and Keryma, sat bleaching away deserted under the constant, unforgiving sun.

The collapse of the nitrate market drained life out of Iquique. But the buildings were still there to remind the young Pinochet couple of the former wealth – a municipal theatre, a Spanish club in the Moorish style and the fading palaces of the nitrate barons. But there was also hunger and lack of supplies in the town and the queues formed early outside the bakeries. Some families queued through the night and in the morning sold their places to the highest bidder as a way of supplementing their income.

When Pinochet arrived Iquique was seven days by boat from Valparaiso or three days by train. There was little electricity or water and hardly any drains. He was comforted in this eerie landscape, he recalls, by the presence of his horse Rex.

Pinochet's duties involved patrolling the desert. On one patrol two of his trucks broke down. His little unit got to the town of Calama at 1.30am when the temperature was two or three degrees below zero, found a place to stay but no food. They were rescued from hunger by a chance encounter with the mayor of the town, Ernesto Meza.

The precariousness and poverty of his early army life in Iquique sits in stark contrast to the great wealth the Pinochet family later acquired from the area. After the 1973 coup the Pinochet family was to prosper hugely from shares in a privatised company, Soquimich, which mined iodine and lithium from this desert.

For the moment, though, life was difficult. In Iquique he almost lost his son Augusto when he swallowed a tube of aspirins and nearly died. Captain Pinochet, now consumed with ambition and a workaholic, spent at least three hours in private study every day to qualify for the Academy of War, the army's staff college. The effort led him to a nervous collapse, and he had to take ten days rest.

One day, just before he travelled down to Santiago to take his entry examination for the Academy, his wife Lucía demonstrated her mettle and her unshakeable belief in her husband. He came home to find the dining room furniture being taken away. When he asked his wife what was happening she replied, according to him: 'You're going to do well and we'll stay in Santiago in our own house, the money we get will allow us to buy all we've sold in Iquique'.

As his wife forecast, Pinochet was to win his place in the staff college. But before he could take it up he had his first taste of active intervention in politics. He also had his first confrontation with the man whom he was to overthrow a quarter of a century later.

President Gabriel González Videla, a member of the Radical Party which had come to power with Communist help in 1946, turned against his erstwhile political comrades. He banned the Communist Party and decreed its leaders should be locked up. In Iquique the Carampangue Regiment was ordered to arrest the Communists, who had been long identified and listed, and confine them in a camp in Pisagua, a tiny and inhospitable seaside settlement.

Captain Pinochet was given sixty troops and sent to the camp. He picked up his prisoners at Humberstone and drove with them through the night to Pisagua. He did not have a good opinion of his 500 charges, who had previously been less than polite to his regiment in Iquique. 'I remember', he writes of the overnight journey, 'that those same arrogant agitators, violent and rude people who spent their time sowing hatred among Chileans, were totally changed. They didn't say a word and were frightened out of their wits and we had to calm some of them.'

There were however some good Communists. One of them was Mayor Meza of Calama, who had given Pinochet and his unit food when they had arrived in his town and could find nothing to eat. On another occasion Pinochet was surrounded on his own by an angry crowd of prisoners out of sight of his troops and his life was saved by a Communist inmate who had been a senior local government officer. In sharp contrast to his later image as a ruthless leader, some Chilean historians say that at Pisagua Pinochet was in fact too lax with the prisoners.

Not much later a group of congressmen arrived without notice to inspect the camp at Pisagua. Among them was Dr Salvador Allende, a member of that part of the Socialist Party which had rejected González Videla's action. Pinochet writes in his autobiography that he refused them entry. When they insisted, he said he would shoot them if they entered. It is highly unlikely that

21

this part of the story is true and must form part of his anti-Marxism stance which the General sedulously invented after the coup, but of which there was no sign before September 1973.

Allende, as Pinochet admits, never recalled it and it is unlikely that an officer of Pinochet's low seniority would have dared threaten death to a member of congress. What is more likely is that he complained to his superiors that the more experienced Communists were turning his camp into a Marxist-Leninist university for the younger comrades and was told he could confiscate Marxist literature.

In 1948 the 32 year-old Pinochet successfully entered the Academy of War as the youngest student of his intake. But there was a last-minute hitch – having done so well against the left at Pisagua, he recounts, he was sent off to do a similar job in another part of the country and told he would go to the Academy later. Another, and perhaps more accurate, version which circulated among those who suspect Pinochet's version of history was that he was not a success at Pisagua and he was sent off south as something of a punishment.

The job was to help impose a state of emergency among miners, many of them Communists, in the coal region of Coronel, not far from Concepción – a curiously similar activity to that of his champion Margaret Thatcher against Arthur Scargill and the British coal miners in the 1980s in Britain.

He settled himself into Coronel and set about clamping what was effectively military rule on a town in ferment. Once, as the miners were being called together by their union to vote on strike action, he called together a group of them for whom he had done favours and told them to station themselves at different points in the meeting hall. When the miners' leader called for the vote they were to shout 'We don't want a strike.' The stratagem succeeded and the leader sought to close the meeting. But Pinochet, according to his own account, strode up to him and said he would be reported to the authorities for having tried to impose a strike. The man desisted and accepted the vote.

In his memoirs he recounts his first impressions of Coronel. 'The sight which most affected me was the state of the miners' housing, their recreation facilities and the way they lived. Such was the state of abandon, hopelessness and indigence of those Chilean workers that one was angered and embittered.'

22

But, far from blaming the mine owners, he had a novel explanation for the conditions. 'It was as breeding ground for the local communists. The bad conditions were made worse by the Marxists themselves so as to take advantage of the resulting poverty and accentuate among the men a consciousness of class differences that would help (the Marxists) to exploit them politically. There was not a moment's respite in the propaganda which aimed to sow hatred among those tough miners and their families.' That opinion, too, could well be part of Pinochet's later reinvention of himself as an anti-Communist.

In his memoirs, Pinochet, no doubt conscious of the need to maintain his reputation for foxiness, tells one incident from this time with relish. The Schwager mine in Coronel had been flooded with pamphlets bitterly critical of the government. The carabineros, the khaki-clad members of the national armed police force, and the personnel of Investigaciones, the plain clothes detective force, had had difficulty in identifying and halting the flow of material. They felt, however, that it could come into Schwager only by train.

Detectives eventually noticed that a middle-aged woman named Luzmila habitually came in on the train from Concepción which arrived at 11.30am, returning on the 5.30pm train. She always carried two baskets in flour sacks. From the baskets she started selling bread on the station and went on alone into town. Pinochet ordered her to be brought to the Investigaciones office. There amid much protests that she was being stopped from earning an honest livelihood for her children Doña Luzmila's baskets were searched and two or three thousand pamphlets found under the bread. The job was now to identify her contacts. She said she was carrying the pamphlets as a favour for a man she hardly knew called Luis and these were collected from her at Coronel.

In the middle of the interrogation Pinochet suddenly told her to take off her ring, which she did after much protest. Inside was engraved the name of the secretary of the Schwager miners' union, a man called Cid. He was rapidly arrested at the union office but he protested that he had never even heard of Luzmila. Then Pinochet told him to take off his ring where the name of Luzmila, who was his wife, was engraved. Neither would own up, or recognise the other. After their arrest, however, the supply of pamphlets was reduced to a trickle.

23

He returned to the Academy after a year at the coal mines, and after three years training finally obtained staff officer status in 1951. He was posted to the Military School through which he himself had passed nearly two decades previously as an officer cadet. There, besides teaching the cadets his specialised subjects he edited a magazine for officers, *Cien Aguilas*, (A Hundred Eagles) which allowed him to make contact with like-minded colleagues in other American armies.

At this time also, he claims, his worries about Marxism began anew. What is certain is that at the Military School he first came to know Manuel Contreras, who became his adjutant and who was to be his staunchest ally and friend for many years. From 1953 until 1972 Pinochet also produced five books on geopolitics, geography and military history almost certainly with Contreras' help. In none of them is there to be found any party political opinions, anti-communist or pro-communist. They are essentially mediocre and have the tone of being written by a studious, slightly grey officer who, as he was later to confess, was surprised to reach the heights he eventually attained.

Afterwards came two years duty in the Rancagua regiment in Arica on the often tense border with Peru. Arica had earned itself a crucial place in Chilean military history. The most northerly town of Chile, it is overshadowed by the Morro, a great fortified rock which was the site of one of Chile's most famous battles. Today, this enormous granite face and the massive Chilean flag which flies over it are illuminated every evening. That was not the case when Pinochet was in the garrison but the rock was always a symbol of Chilean valour.

Arica was the scene of the most desperate land battle in the War of the Pacific. On 7 June 1880, the city, situated in what was then southern Peru, had been heavily fortified and awaited the attack of the Chilean army. A Peruvian garrison of 1,969 soldiers under the command of Colonel Bolognesi occupied the 140-metre high Morro, surrounded by minefields and three forts. The Peruvians were reinforced by an ironclad warship the *Manco Capac*, in the bay.

The Chilean force of 4,379 men was commanded by General Baquedano. It was the Chileans' luck that they captured a Peruvian sapper who had a map of the minefields. Even so, fighting with sword and bayonet was fierce but in the end the Morro was captured to the sound of exploding mines, and Colonel Bolognesi was killed. Seven hundred Peruvians and 473 Chileans lay dead, hundreds more wounded. The captain of the Manco Capac scuttled his vessel and surrendered. The Peruvian flag came down, never to fly in Arica again. There was much for the budding military historian, geopolitician and intelligence expert to muse on in Arica.

At the time the town had 18,000 inhabitants and was, as it remains, dependent on smuggling and various duty-free regulations. American cigarettes, Scotch whisky, French perfumes and Spanish brandy were commonplace contraband at the time Pinochet was posted there. Crossing the border into the Peruvian town of Tacna was easy, but Pinochet recounts how on one occasion he was challenged by a Peruvian border guard because of the frequency of his visits to Peru. He was, after all, head of operations and intelligence for his regiment.

Pinochet was called back to Santiago in 1955 and given the job of Professor of Military Geography and Geopolitics at the Academy of War and a parallel post at the Academy of Air War. Simultaneously he started a law degree at the University of Chile. Within a few months his new postings gave Pinochet his first sight of the corridors of power. He was taken on as assistant to a colonel who was under-secretary of war and started working directly with politicians who would, as he would later recount with disdain, constantly ask favours for themselves or for their supporters.

It was perhaps at this time that his taste for superstition and soothsayers began to develop. He came to wear a ruby ring with his astrological sign (Sagittarius) engraved on it. He also accepted what the wife of a fellow officer told him, that five was his lucky number. On the wall of his office was later to hang the framed copy of Military Proclamation Number 5 which decreed a state of 'internal war' in Chile. The plebiscite he called in 1988 was held on the fifth day of the tenth month, and he always took pains to wear his cap five centimetres higher on his head than those of his fellow officers.

Foreign postings

'With good reason do the people of the US despise
Latin Americans.'
Augusto Pinochet, *Camino Recorrido*

The armed forces gave Major Pinochet an opportunity for foreign travel, albeit limited to the hemisphere. In 1956 he was plucked out to join a group of officers with the job of organising a War Academy in Quito. The ensuing three-and-a-half years spent in the Ecuadorean capital afforded him a chance of living geopolitics at first hand.

Ecuador was an ally of Chile because both had indifferent relations with Peru. Peru, vanquished and occupied by Chile in the 1830s and during the War of the Pacific, as we have seen, had no love for Chileans, who had stolen Peru's Atacama desert and its mineral riches. For its part Ecuador was in conflict with Peru over the latter's possession of vast swathes of the Amazonian jungle.

There had been a brief war between the two countries in 1940 after which a boundary line was traced on the map, called the Rio Protocol. Chile joined Argentina, Brazil and the United States in the job of guaranteeing the border, which stretched from the coast over the cloud-covered Andean peaks and into the Amazonian jungles which were at that time impenetrable to anything but a canoe and impossible to survey with any accuracy. Within thirty days of his arrival, however, Major Pinochet had reconnoitred the country from the Pacific to the Amazon basin and much of the high volcanic Andes which separate the two low-lying regions of the country.

In 1959 Pinochet went on a prolonged tour of the United States with Ecuadorean students from the War Academy. At this time the Pentagon was beginning to develop closer relations than ever with the armies of Latin America. The foundations for this closer relationship had already been well laid. In July 1945 a joint memorandum of the State, War and Navy Departments of the United States said that military aid to the region would involve, 'the indoctrination, training and equipment of the armed forces of the other American republics'.

The 1950s and 1960s saw a tide of political conservatism overtake domestic politics in the United States and elsewhere in the region. In 1954 a socially progressive government in Guatemala was overthrown by the Guatemalan military acting with the support and finance of the CIA and the authorisation of the Eisenhower administration. The next major challenge to the hemispheric status quo was the Cuban revolution in 1959. After Fidel Castro had successfully assumed power in Cuba, Washington gave a new urgency to the fashioning of a relationship with the military of the rest of the region. In 1961 President John Kennedy approved the US-backed ill-fated invasion of Cuba at the Bay of Pigs, which counted on a force of US-supplied Cuban exiles. (Richard Bissell, the CIA officer who had been in charge of the Agency's overthrow of the Guatemalan government in 1954 was given the task of co-ordinating the Bay of Pigs operation seven years later.) In 1964 the left-wing civilian government of Brazil was overthrown by the military. A year later the US sent a force of its own troops, assisted by small contingents from the Brazilian and Paraguayan military dictatorships, to the Dominican Republic to prevent the re-establishment in the presidency of left-winger Juan Bosch. He won free and fair elections in 1962 but had been overthrown by a military coup seven months after taking office.

Writing in his diary on 19 November 1973, two months after the Chilean coup, General Carlos Prats, Pinochet's senior officer and patron summed up how the US government had imbued the Chilean forces with the idea that the Chilean national interest was in fact the US national interest.

'As far as the internal enemy is concerned the opinion acquired by those who have attended courses at the School of the Americas and others organised by the Pentagon has been increasingly prevalent. In 1973 there were already in the Chilean army more than 3,000 personnel who had attended those courses. Many of these (soldiers) have responded to the stereotypes and thoughts which were inculcated into them during these courses and, believing they were liberating the country from the "internal enemy", have committed a crime which can only be explained by their ingenuousness, their ignorance and their political short-sightedness.'

By the time of Pinochet's coup the political views of the US had been so well disseminated among the Chilean armed forces that it was too late to alter the outlook of the majority.

'I imagined,' Prats continued, 'armed forces which were deeply patriotic, aware of the problems and the desires of their people and bound up with them. I used to tell the president that we should send our officers to know what it was like in the countries of Europe, Africa and Asia, not so as to copy or imitate their armed forces but so that they should widen their horizons and understand that the world does not begin or end in the schools of the Pentagon.'

As a middle-ranking officer serving in the 1950s and 60s, Pinochet would have been well aware of the growing US influence in the Chilean armed forces. One Chilean air force officer who underwent training at a US base in Panama in the 1970s said afterwards that 40 per cent of training time was given over to political matters. On his course, he recalled, the lecturers included a Spanish priest and Franco supporter named Father Alejandro and US officers who had served in Vietnam.

During his time in Quito, Pinochet and his Ecuadorean students were invited to the United States, where they were given instruction and introduced to new types of equipment and weapons. In Washington they visited the Pentagon, then went on to New York, calling in at Fort Bliss at El Paso on the border with Mexico before continuing to Dallas and Miami. The contrast between the cleanliness, order and care reigning at El Paso and the dirty, impoverished Ciudad Juárez on the Mexican side of the Rio Grande impressed him. 'Seeing those differences with good reason do the people of the United States despise Latin Americans', he wrote in his memoirs.

In January 1965 there was another trip to the United States, this time with the third-year students at the Academy of War. Photographs from this time show Pinochet with the Chilean students at Fort Benning and at a ceremony with a US general at the School of Artillery. At Fort Leavenworth he called in on Chilean military undergoing training and in company with a US colonel he had come to know he visited Dallas, a gleaming oil-boom city, whose prosperity and development left a lasting impression.

The Vietnam war was at its height and, Pinochet claims, on many occasions when he was called on to make a speech he underlined the valour of US soldiers who were fighting for democracy. In one town he noticed the flags flying at half -mast outside some houses. He stopped his car outside and asked, through his interpreter, if he could chat with the family of the fallen serviceman. In his memoirs he recalls how he spoke with an aged lady whose grandson had been killed in action. He expressed his condolences on behalf of the Chilean officers. She hugged him and thanked him.

General Pinochet

'To reach that rank fulfilled one of my greatest desires'
Augusto Pinochet, *Camino Recorrido*

Back in Chile, Major Pinochet was given a succession of promotions. First he was posted to the staff of the First Division in Antofagasta. The next year he received his first important command when he was chosen to head the Esmeralda regiment. Three years later he was appointed deputy director of Chile's War Academy and in 1968 he was promoted to brigadier-general in command of the Sixth Division based in Iquique.

In the same year Pinochet was given a more political appointment. By now Pinochet was learning to sniff the air of politics and had tentatively expressed support for President Frei Montalva's ruling Christian Democratic Party. To show sympathy with the party in power was likely to aid his career and it probably landed him the job of *subintendente* or deputy regional governor of Tarapacá, a post which gave him responsibility for some civilian matters as well as his strictly military duties. It was a sign that the authorities far to the south in Santiago had confidence in him. He continued to occupy the post after Salvador Allende came to power in 1970.

Because of his duties, both civilian and military, Pinochet was absent in the north hundreds of kilometres away from the capital as politics in Chile started down the road which was to lead the country to cataclysm.

A new president, a self-confessed Marxist, had been constitutionally voted into office in free and fair elections. He was committed to transforming Chilean society in a way which would favour its poorer members by redistributing wealth and land.

The prospect understandably sent a shudder through wealthier Chileans. It was seen in the US capital for what it was: a rejection of Washington's aspirations set out at the beginning of the nineteenth century, well before Karl Marx's views gained currency, to direct the policies of governments throughout the hemisphere. Conservatives in Chile and conservatives in the United States started coming together to stop Salvador Allende.

The Chilean right, President Richard Nixon, Secretary of State Henry Kissinger and US companies with investments in Chile such as the International Telephone and Telegraph Corporation (ITT) sought to prevent Allende assuming the presidency to which he had been elected on 4 September 1970. On 15 September Nixon called a meeting attended by Kissinger, Attorney General John Mitchell and CIA director Richard Helms. He demanded a military coup to keep Allende from office, one which would be engineered by the US government but kept secret from the State Department and the Department of Defence, both of which the President regarded as unreliable.

Helms' notes, later revealed, read,

One in 10 chance perhaps, but save Chile!
worth spending
not concerned risks involved
no involvement of embassy
$10,000,000 available, more if necessary
full-time job – best men we have
game plan
make the economy scream
48 hours for plan of action

The United States ambassador in Santiago, Edward Korry, may not have been involved directly in Nixon's secret plan, but he knew which way his country's leadership was veering. He was merciless about Allende's prospects . In a report on 21 September to Kissinger the ambassador said, 'Once Allende comes to power we shall do all within our power to condemn Chile and the Chileans to utmost deprivation and poverty.'

Chile had already been the scene of quiet political intervention by successive US governments. Though many Chilean Christian Democrats were unaware of the fact, Washington's chosen instrument over the years was the Chilean Christian Democrat Party. It was seen by definition as being anti-communist, cautiously reformist in a region where vast inequalities in society desperately needed reform, yet friendly to business and not excessively hostile to US global strategies.

A similar strategy had been employed in Italy in the years following the end of the Second World War, when, with British and US help, the Christian Democrat Party had done valuable work in preventing a popular Communist Party from getting close to power in Rome. Now in Latin America Christian Democracy was able to play a similar role, co-operating in the Alliance for Progress and presenting to Chileans and Latin Americans generally an alternative to the left-wing nationalism of Fidel Castro.

With their own popularity bolstered with massive funds secretly provided from Washington, the Christian Democrats had swept into power in 1964. (In his book, *Soberanos e Intervenidos: estrategias globales, americanos y españoles*, Juan Garcés shows how in 1962 US agencies gave the Christian Democrats $50,000 for their campaign and a further $180,000 to their presidential candidate, Eduardo Frei Montalva, personally, and how the CIA and the Agency for International Development helped finance the pro-Frei activities of the Belgian Jestuit, Roger Vekemans, which employed 100 people and cost up to $30 million a year to run.) Their cautious leader, Eduardo Frei Montalva, the descendant of immigrants from Switzerland, won an outright majority of 56 per cent in an election which the party termed 'an earthquake'. They expected to stay in power for decade to put into practice what they called their 'Revolution in Liberty'. In the event Frei's caution prevented them from carrying out the platform on which they had been elected.

In the 1970 presidential elections the voters took their revenge. The Christian Democrat candidate Radomiro Tomic came a poor third, gaining 27.8 per cent of the vote, only half the percentage that Eduardo Frei Montalva had won in 1964. Instead they voted for the Popular Unity candidate, the bespectacled veteran of Chilean politics. On 5 November 1970, Salvador Allende delivered his inaugural address to the people as President of Chile.

31

The 1,000 days presidency: the rise of Salvador Allende

Like Pinochet, Salvador Allende was born in Valparaiso. His father was a lawyer and a member of the Radical Party, the traditional party of the professional middle classes. Allende was an excellent student in his secondary school, the Liceo Eduardo de la Barra. He liked to play sports and in these years met a figure who was to influence his political ideas, the Italian anarchist Juan Demarchi, who introduced the young Allende to seminal Marxist works.

In 1925 he went on to perform his military service, and later to officially join the Army reserves. The next year he entered the University of Chile in Santiago to study medicine. Three years later, in 1929, he became a freemason, following a family tradition. By 1930 he had developed a taste for politics – no doubt encouraged by his position as the vice-president of the Federation of Students of Chile. Along with other students he demonstrated against the dictatorship of Carlos Ibáñez.

In the 1930s he practised medicine in his home town of Valparaiso, where he had returned to be near his ailing father. In June of 1932 the dictatorship fell, and the Socialist Republic of Marmaduke Grove was declared. After Grove was deposed, the new government cracked down on 'progressive elements', and Allende was sent to jail. During his time in prison his father died. The young doctor swore, on the tomb of his father, to dedicate his life to the fight for liberty in Chile.

By 1935, now a fully qualified doctor, he was Director of the Chilean Medical Association. He also participated in the creation of a new political grouping, the Popular Front, becoming its provincial president in Valparaiso.

On a hot summer night in 1939 one of the periodic earthquakes that plagued Valparaiso struck; this was the night that Allende met his future wife, a history teacher from Santiago, Hortensia Bussi Soto to whom he was to remain married, though for many years estranged, until his death.

By 1942 he was the Secretary General of the Socialist Party of Chile. Three years later he had won a seat in the Senate. When the Socialist Party split in two factions in 1947, Allende threw in his lot with the more radical Popular Socialist Party, opposed to the policies of President Gabriel Gonzalez Videla, who outlawed the Communist Party. The next year he made his visit to the political prisoners, interned in the camp at Pisagua – at the time under the command of one Captain Pinochet.

In 1952 Allende made the first of his four attempts to win the presidency of his country, as the candidate of the Popular Action Front, the FRAP. He obtained 52,000 votes in an election won by the former military dictator Ibáñez, a man who had mellowed, won some popular esteem and finally achieved his longstanding ambition of being elected to the presidency of his country rather than seizing it.

Allende was much better travelled than Pinochet by the time in their lives when events brought them in direct conflict with one another. Besides his trips to South American countries and to the United States as President of the Chilean Medical Association, in the 1950s he also visited France, Italy, the Soviet Union and the People's Republic of China. In the late 1960s he went to Vietnam, Cambodia and Laos.

While Pinochet the soldier was something of an introverted and grey workoholic with little charisma, Allende the politician was an outgoing bon viveur, a witty man, sometimes inclined to bouts of irascibility, but someone who clearly enjoyed life. He appreciated good food and wine and was sufficiently confident of his own personality to be able to indulge in occasional excursions into self-deprecation. Having first met him at a dinner party in Santiago in 1966, during his presidency I was several times invited to the Moneda. During one particularly tense time in 1973 a small group of us were dining in the palace when he turned to me and exclaimed with a laugh, 'Does this look like the Last Days of Pompeii?'

While Pinochet was clearly uneasy in middle-class society, Allende could hold his own in any company. Pinochet displayed a distinct prudishness, but Allende was a sparkling personality. He was familiarly known as *El Chicho*, a Chilean term for those with reddish curly hair. In his middle age he formed a long-lasting liaison with his secretary, Miriam Rupert, nicknamed *La Payita*.

At the same time, somewhat in contrast to this image of the refined bon-viveur, Allende was a hands-on politician, tirelessly campaigning the length and breadth of the country, picking up shovels and working side by side with the workers, and speaking eloquently to his chosen constituency. He told Chileans he wanted to be their first *compañero presidente*, a president who would be their friend, colleague and equal.

In 1965 he was chosen as the best parliamentarian by the political editors of the Chilean dailies and the next year he became President of the Chilean Senate. In 1969 he oversaw the creation of the Popular Unity coalition of parties, a complex coalition of Communists, Socialists, Radicals, the tiny API, the centrist Social Democrats and the MAPU which had splintered off from the Christian Democrats. On 22 January 1970 the coalition declared his candidacy for the presidency of the republic.

He faced two main rivals, Radomiro Tomic, the aspiring heir to Frei's Christian Democratic mantle and former President Jorge Alessandri, the candidate of the recently established National Party, a fusion of the Conservative Party and the no less conservative Liberal Party. Both candidates were figures who harked back to Chile's unsatisfactory past but had their parties come together to present a single candidate. Allende presented a platform of change. In the event he sneaked home winning 36.2 per cent of the vote to the 34.9 per cent won by Alessandri. The Christian Democratic vote slumped, Tomic winning exactly half the proportion Frei had done in 1964.

In Washington, alarm bells began to ring and plans for a US sponsored coup aimed at preventing Allende from taking office were mooted. Among wealthier Chileans their support was for an immediate US-sponsored military coup to prevent Allende acceding to power. The main obstacle to a military coup of the kind that had been mounted with US assistance against elected governments in Guatemala in 1954 was General René Schneider, the army commander-in-chief. Schneider was loyal to the principle that the Chilean armed forces should support the elected government and stand aside to let party politics take their course. He became the main target of those in Chile and in the United States who wanted the army to unite with the Christian Democrats to prevent the accession of Allende to the presidency.

On election day two-thirds of Chileans had voted against the socialist project. With only 36 per cent of the vote the decision of who was to become the new president had to be taken in a plenary session of both houses of Congress. This offered an opportunity to

Allende's enemies to get together a congressional majority to block his confirmation.

In *Soberanos e Intervenidos* Garcés quotes a US Senate report of 1975 on how, on 14 September, the US government gave Frei $250,000 with which to bribe Chilean parliamentarians to vote against the confirmation.

On 22 October, as the Congress gathered in plenary session to decide on who was to be successor to Eduardo Frei, Schneider was shot by right-wing Chileans. Later it emerged that there had been an US-sponsored plan to kill Schneider. A US military attaché, Colonel Paul Wimert, was later to confess he carried down from Washington another large sum in dollar banknotes – which he said he kept in his riding boots. But it was not needed; the deed had already been done.

Schneider died three days later in the military hospital in Santiago. The assassination was aimed at spreading terror and panic but it had the opposite effect: Schneider had been a popular figure, and an officer; there was an expression of popular revulsion at the crime. For his part Pinochet noted in his memoirs his pleasure that the dead Schneider had been replaced by his long-standing friend and comrade-in-arms, General Carlos Prats.

On 24 October, as Schneider was still fighting in vain for his life, Allende was declared president-elect by Congress. He assumed the presidency on 3 November, accepting the presidential sash of office from the incumbent, Eduardo Frei Montalva. Hope for the left was kindled once again. For Allende it was the culmination of a political career begun forty years previously.

Economy and class in the Chile of 1970

At the time Salvador Allende came to power in 1970, Chile had one of the best organised working classes in Latin America. In the preceding decades, as people fled the countryside, it had become a largely urbanised nation, with more than 70 per cent of the population living in cities or towns.

Chilean workers had a history of engaging in political struggle and mounting opposition to various governments when they felt their interests were threatened – a propensity which had brought it into brutal contact with the military. In one of the largest massacres of civilians in recent South American history, in 1907, 3,000 striking miners and their families were killed by troops after a demonstration in the nitrate stronghold of Iquique.

At the same time, by 1970, Chile also had a powerful parliamentary democracy, bounded by conventions, a constitution, and what could be called a 'democratic culture'. While successive military-sponsored regimes appeared and fell with regularity in neighbouring countries, Chile proudly thought of itself as 'the England of Latin America'.

Even during the period of military dictatorship from 1924-1931 repression took the form of imprisonment and exile rather than torture and outright murder.

In the halls of Congress and power a conservative political tradition prevailed. Despite Allende's victory in the race for the presidency, the parties of Popular Unity were in a minority in the Senate and the House of Representatives as compared to the forces of the right. The right was to make great use of its congressional majority to try and stymie Allende at every turn.

While Chile might have had a solid political democracy, the economy was precarious. The Chile of 1970 was hugely dependent on foreign exports of its abundant raw materials – particularly copper. Even minor shifts in international markets for the minerals and foodstuffs it produced could produce a major change in domestic economic fortunes. This structural economic vulnerability haunted Chile – and still does, to an extent. Some historians of Chile believe there would never have been a military dictatorship in the 1920s if the international nitrates market had not collapsed due to the invention of artificial nitrates after the First World War. Similarly, when the Great Depression caused the total value of Chile's exports to fall by 88 per cent – the steepest decline in the world – the dictatorship of Ibáñez fell.

By 1970 it was still the case that a single shift in world markets for one of Chile's primary products could, theoretically, rupture the country's entire social structure – a situation Roxborough, O'Brien and Roddick in their book *Chile: the State and Revolution*, published a year after the coup, describe as 'a singularly ill-balanced economy and society'. It was one of the Allende government's several strokes of bad luck that the price of copper fell on world markets between 1970 and 1972.

Chilean working people were frustrated by the constant flux in their conditions brought about by the influence of powerful foreign interests. The Chilean middle class, for their part, harboured resentment toward the tiny tranche of wealthy Chileans who controlled much of the import-export and external financial trades. What the experiment of Salvador Allende showed was that while the Chilean middle classes might have felt resentful toward the economic elite, they were unwilling to 'accept socialism with a patriotic face'. Under the threat of revolution, the middle and upper classes reacted defensively, one could even say hysterically, in the face of the socialist arguments for redistribution of wealth in the name of the national good and equality for all.

Once in power, the divisions Allende faced within his own ranks were as problematic as anything he faced from his opponents in Congress. Allende's Socialist Party resisted the principle of 'democratic centralism' the sort of dictatorship of the party bosses which was the norm in the Soviet Union, China and elsewhere. The Socialists never achieved the sort of discipline which, for instance, the more Stalinist Communist Party achieved. They were also at odds with the extreme left, who favoured a more 'revolutionary', meaning violent, if necessary, transition to Communism.

Besides differing political views, there was considerable personal antipathy between the membership of the Socialists and the Communists. The Communists declared the Socialists humdrum characters, authoritarian and unadventurous. For their part Socialists thought of the Communists as hot-headed and hasty. Both were able to agree on their broad objective to transform society into something more equitable but a consensus on the ways of achieving was difficult if not impossible to find. While many in the government wanted measures to curb what had become a situation of chronic inflation, others saw the encouragement of inflation as a splendid way of weakening the bourgeois state. The job of co-ordination among the parties would have taxed the cleverest political leader.

At the time of Allende's accession, a small elite was in charge of an economy, where, as in the rest of Latin America, the majority had few economic rights. As the head of a popular government dedicated to improving the lot of working people, Allende's task was to immediately and successfully challenge the status quo.

37

In his victory speech in the National Stadium on 5 November 1970, Allende proclaimed:

... we shall abolish the pillars propping up that minority that has always condemned our country to under-development. We shall abolish the monopolies which grant control of the economy to a few dozen families. We shall abolish a tax system which favours profiteering and which has always put a greater burden on the poor than the rich. We are going to nationalise credit. We shall abolish the large estates which condemn thousands of peasants to serfdom. We shall put an end to the foreign ownership of our industry and our sources of employment.

The road to socialism lies through democracy, pluralism and freedom. Because of its particular conditions the social and political institutions are available to in Chile to realise the transition from backwardness and dependence to development and autonomy in a socialist way.

In a word, Salvador Allende had just proclaimed that Chile was to progress towards a state of left-wing social democracy, comparable to what Clement Attlee had aspired to in Britain, Willy Brandt was pursuing in Germany and François Mitterrand was to seek in France. There was no aspiration to a Stalinist or Maoist communist dictatorship.

In his first message to congress in May 1971 Allende declared 'We recognise the political freedom of the opposition and we will conduct all our activities with the terms of the constitution. Political freedom is the prized possession of all Chilean people.'

He rejected violence. Transformation of society he promised 'will come about without the use of unnecessary physical coercion, without institutional disorder and without disorganising production, at a pace set by the government in accordance with the needs of the people and the development of our resources.'

During the first days of the new government wealthy Chileans were split on how to respond to the challenge from Allende and the growing power of organised labour. As the murder of Schneider showed, some wanted Allende's blood, on the other side of the divide were businessmen, wealthy families and opposing politicians who felt unwilling to overthrow the government, but who were keen to use every other means of destabilisation at their disposal to bring about its downfall.

Just after Popular Unity came to power the United States Ambassador Edward Korry sent a cable to President Nixon. It is interesting for its frank appreciation of the attitudes of the Chilean right:

> I have confessed repeatedly in these communications my equal distrust of a right that blindly and greedily pursued its interest, wandering in a myopia of arrogant stupidity. They disdained organisation and deliberately scorned the one element of their forces that had some semblance of structure, the National Party. They preached vengeance against the Christian Democrats, whom they regarded as a more justifiable enemy because of its betrayal of class rather than the Communists. They forgot the first rule of nature, of change, and insolently believed that time stands still. They only tolerated a few modernists in their midst, men who were certainly no less rich, no less self-indulgent, but who at least understood the flux in which we are all caught.

Allende's term of office started well. The first year of his government was accompanied by a great rise in national prosperity. Between 1970 and 1973 Popular Unity noticeably shifted the balance of wealth away from the elite who lived off interest, dividends, and rents, and toward those who lived off wages and salaries. The rich were expected to take taxpaying seriously for the first time.

In a statement made only a month after the government came into office it declared, 'it is necessary to establish a remunerations policy for 1971 which will bring about improvement of the living standards of the workers, especially those who have the lowest remuneration and those who lack stable jobs'. The minimum industrial wage was raised by 66.7 per cent at a time when prices were rising at around 35 per cent a year. The economy expanded by a massive 8.1 per cent in 1971 and even managed a rise of 1.6 per cent in 1972. More poorly paid workers received special bonuses. A feel-good factor suffused the nation. Publishing and the arts flourished and every schoolchild was given a daily glass of milk.

But less than a year after he took office Allende made a move which enraged the Nixon administration. The state took control of the principal copper mines, an action which for years had had support from many different corners of the political spectrum. Copper was still Chile's major export and foreign exchange earner. On 11 July 1971 the Chilean copper mines were nationalised, effectively taking them away from the US multinationals Kennecott and Anaconda. This was done through a parliamentary process which had the enthusiastic support of the government and the Christian Democratic opposition alike. The government provided compensation to the US-based companies, taking into account 'excess profits' made by the two multinationals over the previous 15 years. In September the government announced that these profits had been so high that they exceeded the present value of the mines and therefore there would be no payment forthcoming. In retaliation Nixon announced that the US government would withhold its support for loans under consideration in multinational development banks.

Meanwhile, opposition was intensifying on other fronts. The more right-wing of the political parties used their parliamentary majority to do their best to halt Allende's social plans. On the left he faced the contempt of the Movement of the Revolutionary Left, the MIR, which was impatient with Allende's loyalty to the constitution.

It must also be remembered that these were the times of the Cold War. Allende's opponents abroad were fearful that, whatever Allende's intentions, a Communist dictatorship would eventually be established, one which would give the USSR a new base in the South Pacific. Western investments would suffer and US hegemony would be challenged. Henry Kissinger announced the following to a Congressional hearing in Washington a few days after Allende's victory: 'I don't think we should delude ourselves that an Allende takeover in Chile would not present massive problems for us, and for the democratic forces and for pro-US forces in Latin America, and indeed to the whole of the Western Hemisphere'.

Though not directly involved in political matters, Pinochet, with his background in intelligence, must have been aware of the rage of the Chilean right and the disappointment of the US at Allende's accession to power. From the right-wing media came a torrent of criticism directed at the government, notably from the principal

Santiago daily *El Mercurio*, owned by the Edwards family empire, which also controlled a large bank, the main brewery, a half share with Unilever in a big detergent business, and a bottler of Pepsi-Cola.

In January 1971, still the very early days of Allende's new government, Pinochet was called to the capital. He claims in his memoirs that he was fearing dismissal, but this was unlikely, and he states this most likely as part of his attempt to construct an image of a soldier destined to fight and annihilate the left. In fact Pinochet was one of the very first officers promoted by the Popular Unity government, a sign that the new president and his friend General Prats had confidence in his loyalty. In his memoirs he reproduces the card on which one of the Allende government's political intelligence services had kept details and opinions about him. Below his personal details such as home address and the name of his wife and children is the comment,

'Iquique. He is trustworthy – He may well become Commander in Chile – Is well liked by officers and men.'

Santiago days

'I believe that every country has the right to give itself the government it wants'.
Lucía Pinochet Hiriart, daughter of the dictator.

From 1971 onwards the career of this studious, efficient officer became centred on Santiago. As major-general Pinochet was given command of the garrison of the capital. As part of the duties of that post he was involved in the 25-day visit of Fidel Castro to Chile that November and December, including accompanying him to visit the monument to Che Guevara in San Miguel.

In his memoirs Pinochet makes much of the distaste he felt for the Cuban visitor but there is no record from the time that shows he carried out any untoward action. Indeed it may be that Pinochet was responsible for saving Castro's life. Many years later Castro claimed that he had been the target of an assassination attempt while in Chile. The assassins were, he said, men who posed as Venezuelan journalists with Venezuelan credentials and arms supplied from the US embassy in Bolivia which included rifles with telescopic sights, a machine gun and a television camera with a hidden gun.

Given that Pinochet was the senior military man accompanying Allende's guest, he would hardly have been chosen for such a task if his superiors had thought he was unwilling to do the job. Whatever the explanation – another of the many botched US attempts to kill Castro, or the eagle-eyed vigilance of Augusto Pinochet – Castro did not die on Chilean soil. In fact, Allende's confidence in Pinochet was such that he took him the following year on his visit to Mexico, the United Nations, the USSR and Cuba.

More conclusive evidence that Pinochet was trusted was his appointment in January of 1972 as deputy commander-in-chief of the army. This promotion, backed by Prats, would have needed the approval of Allende.

By 1972 the enemies of Allende's unstable coalition of six parties of the left and centre were becoming more desperate in the face of the continuing popularity of Allende, despite the country's difficulties and their own lack of success. In Washington President Nixon and Dr Kissinger were even more committed to the overthrow of the Popular Unity government. In Chile the right was sounding out potential collaborators in the army and in the US.

Despite his later claims, there is no evidence that Pinochet was involved in anti-Allende activities. Speaking on a programme on BBC Radio 4 at the end of June 1999, former US Secretary of State Henry Kissinger said that at the time of the 1973 coup he had no idea who Pinochet was. There is little reason to doubt his word – not least because he has never made any secret of his hostility to the elected government in Chile and of his enthusiasm for the job of subverting it. Nor do official US documents from before the coup so far published refer to Pinochet as a possible leader of a plot against Allende. Kissinger's remarks serve as something of an antidote to the feeling – often encountered on both the left and the right in the US – that Washington's strategies are the determining factor in the politics of other countries.

But to say that Pinochet was never the US candidate to overthrow Allende is not to minimise US attempts at subversion. These included Kissinger's secret '40 Committee' or task force to sabotage the Chilean government; a US$ 1.5 million subsidy for the anti-Allende media; a continuation of the attempts chronicled by Prats to win the military over to a US world view; and many other activities subsequently revealed by the US Congressional investigators and characterised by the US authors of *Death on Embassy Row*, John Dinges and Saul Landau as 'massive covert interference' in Chilean affairs.

Sources of foreign finance dried up – as Richard Nixon had promised when Allende had nationalised the copper mines. In the six years of Eduardo Frei's government Chile received US$302 million from the US government, US$ 192 million from the Inter-American Development Bank and US$98 from the UN World Bank to give a total of US$592 million. During Allende's less than three years in office the corresponding figures were nil, US$11 million, nil and US$11million.

In his address to the UN on 4 December 1972 Allende condemned US action in terms which Fidel Castro was constantly in the habit of using (apart from the reference to elections).

> From the very day of our electoral victory on 4 September 1970, we have felt the effects of a large-scale external pressure against us which tried to prevent the inauguration of a government freely elected by the people, and has attempted to bring it down ever since, an action that has tried to cut us off from the world, to strangle our economy and paralyse trade in our principal export copper, and to deprive us of access to sources of international financing.

By 1972 Allende's opponents had hit on a masterly plan to hurt the government. Road transport was a key industry in this long, thin country with few rail links. Most essential goods were moved up and down the country by road. In October of that year lorry owners started to withdraw their vehicles from service in the remote southern province of Aysén in protest against moves towards nationalisation of the industry. Stoppages spread up and down the country and were backed by encouragement from the right-wing Chilean media, which itself benefited from US government subsidies spasmodically almost to the last days of Allende. Jack Anderson, a US columnist, revealed that the strikes had been backed by ITT, a US multinational with large investments in Chile.

It was as though the nervous system of the economy had been paralysed. It was in part these threats that persuaded Allende that the appointment of military officers to the government could assist him. By demonstrating that the military not only supported but were intimately involved in the Popular Unity government, the President hoped to appease the militant right and persuade it to halt its campaign of sabotage which had quickly extended to power lines and railways.

Although there were strong protests from the left of the Popular Unity and the MIR, senior military were given terms in the cabinet from 1972 onward. General Carlos Prats was one of three generals who were appointed to the cabinet. He was given the interior ministry portfolio on 3 November 1972 and served until February of the next year. Senior officers were also appointed to the management of the new nationalised copper industry.

Despite Popular Unity's many failings, their chronic disunity and US co-operation in economic sabotage, Allende's popularity was maintained – indeed it increased. In the congressional elections of March 1973 Popular Unity increased its share of the vote from the 36 per cent achieved in 1970 to 43.4 per cent. The grudging acceptance of some political attitudes was expressed in the slogan of MAPU, one of the members of the Popular Unity coalition – 'This government may be shit, but at least it's ours.'

During the turbulent years of 1972 and 1973 Pinochet's personal fortunes continued to rise. He had earned the trust and confidence of the Popular Unity government and was sent several times to Moscow to negotiate arms contracts with the Soviets on behalf of the Allende government. (Nikolai Leonov, a former senior officer in the KGB who has extensive knowledge of Latin American affairs, told the author in Moscow in August 1999 that shortly before the coup a multi-million pound consignment of arms negotiated by Pinochet on behalf of the Allende government had been dispatched to Chile from the Soviet Union. It had to be called back on the high seas when the Soviets decided that a coup was imminent and did not want their weapons to fall into the hands of the plotters.)

As a senior general and head of the Santiago garrison, Pinochet and his wife Lucía had the opportunity of mixing socially with many of the highest in the land and the government, notably José (Pepe) Tohá, who was Allende's defence minister for much of 1973. Moy de Tohá, the minister's widow, recounts in Pablo Azócar's *Pinochet: Epitafio para un Tirano* (*Pinochet: Epitaph for a Tyrant*) how, before the coup, Pinochet had never had a bad word for Allende, and in fact expressed anger on one occasion in 1973 when the right-wing Edwards press launched a particularly bitter attack on the government.

In June 1973 Pinochet worked closely with the President after a failed military coup in Santiago. A unit of tanks under the command of Colonel Roberto Souper tried to seized power on behalf of Patria y Libertad, Fatherland and Freedom, an overtly Nazi group which was the successor of similar groups in the Chile of the 1930s. Patria y Libertad had been carrying out acts of sabotage against the government as part of their avowed strategy of increasing political tension and provoking general violence. Pinochet showed impatience when Allende ordered that the affair should be resolved by negotiation and not by sending troops loyal to the government to deal with Souper and his men.

Pinochet's identification with Popular Unity was strengthened in government circles by his friendship with the Tohás. They often visited each others' houses and the Pinochets fell into the custom of going to the Tohás' every Sunday for drinks on the balcony of their house in the Calle Enrique Foster. Shortly after Souper's failed coup Allende moved José Tohá from the defence portfolio. There was a farewell party held in the Pinochets' house in Las Condes. For the occasion it was decorated in red with Japanese knick-knacks arranged on little tables. The party was attended by senior officers and their wives. Afterward the Pinochets sent the following note to the Tohás:

> Lucía and Augusto Pinochet Ugarte, Major General, present their compliments to their distinguished friends Don José Tohá G, and Sra. Victoria E. Morales de Tohá, and thank them very sincerely for their noble gesture of friendship on the occasion of their departure from ministerial duties.
>
> Lucía and Augusto wish to express the deep and affectionate regard they have for the Tohá-Morales couple and ask them to continue to look on them as their friends.
>
> We hope that on Lucía's return we will have the good fortune to enjoy your kind company. Meanwhile be assured, as always, of our fondest good wishes.

Santiago, 10th July 1973

Despite military backing of the government and naming Prats, Admiral Raúl Montero, air force General César Ruiz Denyau and carabinero General José María Sepúlveda for the cabinet the campaign of sabotage, strikes and terror by the right continued. In July-August 1973 twenty people died in political confrontations. There were 71 attacks on trucks whose owners refused to join the road transport strike, 77 against buses and 16 against service stations and 37 against railway lines.

On 13 August right-wing terrorists blew up high-voltage electricity pylons causing blackouts lasting for several hours in eight provinces. In a speech which was itself interrupted by a power failure, Allende commented that had all the planned sabotage of power lines gone ahead the country as a whole would have been without electricity for a month. Chile was beginning to slide into chaos.

Endgame

In his diary entry for 22 August 1973 Carlos Prats remembered Pinochet telling him how he had said to Allende, 'President, be aware that I am ready to lay down my life in defence of the constitutional government that you represent.'

In August 1973 Prats, the symbol of the armed forces' support for the Allende government, was inveigled into an incident in the centre of Santiago. A bespectacled person with short hair gestured at him in a lewd manner as he was being driven to his office by his batman. Prats drew his pistol and pointed it at the person, who turned out to be a woman. A crowd, co-ordinated beforehand, gathered and booed him. On 21 August some three hundred middle-class women, many of them the wives of officers, appeared at his door in the early evening to insult him. As the hours passed the mob grew to around two thousand. Prats called a gathering of officers early the next morning to seek their support, but a majority came out against him. Prats felt he had no alternative but to resign.

On 23 August 1973 Allende named Pinochet commander-in-chief of the army on Prats' departure. General Prats was a friend and comrade-in-arms for many years and had recommended Pinochet to the president as his successor.

Santiago, 7 September 1973

My dear general and friend,

As I succeed you at the head of the body that you commanded with such dignity, I write to convey to you – with my unchanging affection towards you personally – my feelings of sincere friendship, born not only in the course of our careers, but also – very specially – cemented in the delicate circumstances that we have had to face. In writing these lines to you, I do so with the firm conviction that I am addressing not just a friend but above all the general who in the responsibilities he undertook, was lead only by a high sense of responsibility towards the army and the country alike.

It is therefore for me a profound pleasure to express to you, with my greetings and best wishes to you and your lady wife and family for the future, my assurance that I who have succeeded you in command of the army am unconditionally at your service, professionally as well as privately and personally.

With my warm regards,

Augusto Pinochet Ugarte

Letter from Pinochet to General Carlos Prats

III

Treason and Terror

'In trust I have found treason'
Queen Elizabeth I
(1533-1603)

The plot

At the age of fifty-seven Pinochet had achieved many of his ambitions. He was the military master of the country, accepted in government circles and respected among his fellow officers.

Yet even at this late stage Augusto Pinochet was not in the fast-brewing plot to overthrow the legitimate head of state. In the wake of Prats' departure two other senior army generals, Pickering and Sepúlveda, decided to retire, strengthening a group of generals and colonels under the principal plotter General Sergio Arellano Stark.

For his part, Pinochet was reluctant to dismiss generals he did not like, demanding resignations from Generals Arturo Riveros, Pedro Palacios and Arellano but then not following through. Meanwhile Arellano and his group fixed 28 August as the date of the coup, only to later postpone it. So little did Stark's plotters trust Pinochet that they did not tell him of their coup plans. They remained as sceptical as ever of making an approach to the new army commander-in-chief, an apparently close friend and confidant of Prats, a man who had given no signal whatsoever of disloyalty to the President and who could, if approached, have given the whole game away to Allende.

For his part, Allende could not have suspected Pinochet's involvement in seditious plans. Pinochet was considered the armed forces' leading constitutionalist. Popular Unity had let him sit on its own Security Council, which had also allowed Pinochet access to the government's defence plans should an insurrection arise.

49

Calm before the storm

Tension was in the air in the weeks leading up to the coup. The failed takeover by Colonel Souper on 29 June was followed by the assassination of Commander Arturo Araya, Allende's naval aide-de-camp. At the end of July truck owners went on strike again – as they had been doing regularly since the previous year, paralysing distribution of goods throughout the country. Power lines and railway tracks continued to be sabotaged and queues formed at food shops. Dwindling supplies flew off the shelves as people sought to stockpile goods.

In the snug bar of Santiago's Carrera Hotel, foreign journalists gathered every night to swap gossip. Some were apprehensive for the future of democracy in Chile, others exulted as Allende's difficulties mounted, many were inconvenienced by the fact that tonic water was not available, although gin continued to flow abundantly. In the news kiosks the press of the left, the centre and the right battled it out for readership – the Allende government had refused to censor the press. There were daily reports of confrontations between the carabineros and urban workers or peasants as factories and land were seized.

In the days and years after the coup, middle- and upper-class citizens said that they felt their very lives were threatened – that a class war was brewing; indeed it was reported that arms for the left were arriving from Cuba hidden in sugar sacks. The terror campaign predicted by the right failed to appear – only further rationing and inflation. The mass of the population suffered as prices rose at an annual rate of 500 per cent. Paper money had to be spent and converted into goods and services as soon as possible.

A fixed official exchange rate of 350 escudos to the US dollar in September 1973 bore no relationship to the 1,500 escudos it cost to buy one on the black market as Chileans sought dollars at any price. Many journalists – especially television producers responsible for large outlays – made fortunes by charging their employers for expenses in escudos at the official rate of exchange while buying the Chilean currency at a fraction of that cost on the black market.

Everything from fur coats to houses and flats was changing hands for ridiculously small quantities of US dollars as the middle-class sought a stable currency which was capable of being exported.

Despite everything, hundreds of thousands of Chileans filled the streets of the capital on 4 September in a show of support for the government.

Strangely, in the very last days of the Allende government there came a moment of calm. Those journalists who were normally based in Buenos Aires returned to Argentina, cheerily forecasting that they would be back immediately the coup came. Little did they know they would have to wait at the border for many days before they were allowed back in.

Those of us who went about our business in the beatific moment of calm before the storm sensed the strange atmosphere of stasis would be short-lived.

In the back rooms of the military, preparations for the coup continued. In view of Prats continuing loyalty to the government, the senior officers of the navy and the air force shivered at the prospect of trying to pull off a coup on their own. Without Prats on side, if they went ahead they risked confrontation with the army and all-out civil war. Leaders of the fourth arm, the carabineros, decided to go along with the army. As the commanders of the navy and the carabineros shared Prats' loyalty to Allende, the disaffected naval and carabinero officers were starting out on a path of not just treason to the state but mutiny towards their senior commanders.

The die was cast on the evening of Saturday 8 September. At 8.30 in the evening General Arellano said he arrived at Pinochet's house and told him of the plot, a piece of news which left him surprised and troubled. But General Nicanor Díaz Estrada of the air force reported that Arellano told him at the time that he 'never dared' to do such a thing.

At lunchtime on that Saturday, three days before the coup, Allende was visited at home by the newly-retired General Prats who spoke to the President privately. Though Prats' diary is silent about the visit, after their conversation Allende, in grave mood, summoned Pinochet and General Orlando Urbina to a meeting the next day. At lunch on Sunday at the presidential residence Allende revealed to Pinochet that he had decided to announce the holding of a plebiscite on the future of the government. Allende was convinced that a majority in the country would back the elected government, despite the political and economic difficulties into which the country had been plunged.

After lunch with the President Pinochet went home. At about five in the afternoon he and his wife hosted his daughter Jacqueline's birthday party. An unusual guest arrived in the form of General

Gustavo Leigh, recently appointed by Allende commander-in-chief of the air force. Leigh asked Pinochet what he was going to do. According to Leigh, Pinochet was still not decided. 'Have you thought that this might cost us our lives and the lives of many others?' asked Pinochet.

While Pinochet and Leigh talked surrounded by the children's screams of delight, the navy plotters, acting without orders from their commander-in-chief Admiral Montero, arrived from Valparaiso. They were led by Admiral Gustavo Carvajal and included Admiral Huidobro, the commander of the marines, and Captain Ariel González, head of naval intelligence. They bore an important paper from Admiral José Toribio Merino, the chief navy plotter. They too were keen to know which way the army was going to jump.

The paper said:

'9 September 1973,
Gustavo and Augusto:
On my word of honour, H day will be the 11th and H hour will be 06.00. If you cannot carry out this phase with all the forces you control in Santiago explain this on the back. Admiral Huidobro is authorised to treat and discuss any matter with you.
With greetings of hope and understanding, Merino.'

On the back of the paper are less formal notes,

'Gustavo: this is the last opportunity. J.T.'

then

'Augusto: if you don't put all the strength of Santiago from the first moment, we won't be alive to see the future. Pepe.'

Below that again are the words,

'Agreed, Gustavo Leigh'

and

Agreed, A.Pinochet'.

Only the signatures were missing. Leigh signed straight away. Pinochet dithered again. 'If this got out there could be serious consequences for us,' he lamented.

Leigh broke the silence.

'Decide, General. Pull yourself together.'

Augusto Pinochet, the pious little boy who always wanted to be a soldier, signed and under his signature put the stamp of the commander-in-chief.

The way was clear for Leigh to send his Hawker Hunter fighters the day after next to bomb the elected President in his palace.

Blitz

Now committed to the coup d'état, Pinochet had to give the impression of normality. On the morning of Monday the 10th of September he secretly made Generals Brady, Benavides, Arellano and Palacios and Colonel Polloni swear loyalty to the plot on the sword of Captain General Bernardo O'Higgins, the architect of Chilean independence from Spain. He reminded them they could die. If he himself were to die or not to be found at his post he named General Oscar Bonilla to succeed him as head of the army.

At four o'clock General César Mendoza, the third in seniority in the paramilitary police – who only two days before toasted the President at a formal dinner in the School of Carabineros and publicly paid tribute to his courage in 'leading his people along the path to greater social justice' – signed his pledge of loyalty to the plot. The fourth element in the armed conspiracy was in place. At the end of the day Pinochet's chauffeur took him home.

There he told his bodyguards to go off to eat. He played with the dog in the garden and then went for a walk around the block. The house fell into darkness except for the light in his study where he continued working in his usual workaholic manner until eleven-thirty.

Pinochet did not get much sleep that night. On the morning of 11 September he was up at 5.30am to have a shower. An hour later he received a call from Allende's residence, where news had arrived of unusual troop movements. He pretended that he had just woken up and gave an evasive reply, saying he would call back.

Meanwhile Lucía and members of the family were packed off to the headquarters of the mountain troops at Los Andes, 77 kilometres north of the city on the road over the Andes to Argentina. The base was commanded by Colonel Renato Cantuarias, known to be loyal to the government. Pinochet reasoned that Lucía and the children would be in good hands with him were the coup to fail. (The colonel's body was discovered a few days after the coup riddled with bullets. The official version circulated later was that he had killed himself.)

Pinochet set out from his house at 7.10am in convoy for the base at the Santiago suburb of Peñalolén, where he was expected at 7.40. He arrived a little late, causing the chief plotter there, General Bonilla, no little anxiety. He had made a detour to pass by his son Augusto's house to see his sleeping grandchildren, perhaps, he thought, for the last time.

At 7am President Salvador Allende took a telephone call at his home that informed him the navy had rebelled in Valparaiso. He then left directly for the Moneda, the Presidential Palace, accompanied by José María Sepúlveda the Director-General of the Carabineros, about 50 policemen and the group of personal friends who had served as his bodyguard since he assumed the presidency in 1970.

Allende and his entourage had difficulty reaching the palace, which had already been surrounded by police loyal to the Generals. When he finally managed to get inside, Allende was told that the armed forces had also revolted. Via the palace's radio station he broadcast an appeal for the working class to mobilise. In fact, several busloads of workers attempting to get to the palace in a show of support were turned back that morning by troops.

Meanwhile Pinochet had arrived at Peñalolén. There he maintained radio contact with Leigh at the Santiago air base of El Bosque and with Carvajal, who, acting with Merino, had seized control of the navy from the commander-in-chief, Admiral Montero, who was unwilling join the plot. For his part Montero was confined behind the gates of his official house in the capital which were secured with new locks and guarded by troops. His telephone was cut off and his car immobilised. Stupefied, the legitimate commander-in-chief of the navy offered no resistance.

54

The case of General José María Sepúlveda, the legitimate
commander-in-chief of the carabineros overthrown by his junior
General Mendoza, was different. He stayed beside the President in
the Moneda, though all his men deserted.

From Peñalolén Pinochet directed operations in collaboration
with Admiral Merino in Valparaiso, General Leigh at the air force
base at El Bosque and with Admiral Patricio Carvajal at the ministry of defence. Meanwhile, Allende spent several hours of that Tuesday morning worrying about Pinochet's safety in the midst of what
was clearly a full insurrection.

Early that morning the President was presented with an ultimatum
by the coup plotters. It read:

In view of the grave economic, social and moral crisis which
is destroying the country, the inability of the government to
take steps to put an end to the developing chaos, the constant
growth of paramilitary groups organised and trained by Popular
Unity, who are leading the country towards an inevitable civil
war;

The armed forces and police declare that:

The President of the Republic must resign from his high
post immediately, in favour of the armed forces and the police;

The armed forces and the police are united in their
determination to assume their historic role of fighting to free
their country from the Marxist yoke and to re-establish order
and the rule of law;

The workers of Chile may be assured that the social and
economic gains which they have obtained up to now, will not
be subjected to fundamental changes;

Popular Unity press, radio stations and television networks
must suspend their activities immediately. If not, they will be
taken by assault by the army and the air force;

The population of Santiago must remain at home to avoid
the massacre of innocent people.

Signed:
General Augusto Pinochet Ugarte, Commander of the Army.
Admiral José Toribio Merino, Commander of the Navy.
General Gustavo Leigh Guzmán, Commander of the Air Force.
General César Mendoza Durán, Commander of the Police.

Pinochet's name on the communique was perhaps the biggest surprise for the President. Allende's response was, 'Poor Pinochet, he's been captured.'

Once the ultimatum was received, according to Allende's daughter Beatriz, who was with him in the Palace, several of his bodyguards refused to remain with him and fight to the end.

At 8.45am the armed forces bombed one pro-government radio transmitter, putting it off the air. By 9.30am all international telephone connections had been cut, and the last commercial flight to arrive or leave Chile for a week took off from the capital's Pudahuel airport.

At mid-morning Pinochet, through Admiral Gustavo Carvajal, one of the principal navy plotters, telephoned the Moneda Palace to offer the President an aircraft and safe passage for him and his companions into exile.

Allende's reply to the Admiral was trenchant. 'Who do you people think you are, you treacherous shits! Stuff your plane up your arses! You are talking to the President of the Republic! And the President elected by the people doesn't surrender!' he bellowed and slammed down the phone with such force that it jumped back off the hook. The President's chronically high blood pressure went through the roof.

According to evidence given to the Chilean journalist, Mónica González, in September 1999 by Luis Enríquez, who was on duty in the Moneda as a young policeman on that day, a caller from the US embassy also phoned the Moneda urging Allende to accept the military's terms and offering its guarantee of the president's safety.

At 9.30am President Allende broadcast his last message to the nation via Radio Magellanes, the only remaining pro-government station on the air.

Compatriots:

This is certainly the last time I shall speak to you. The air force has bombed all our radio stations. My words flow more from disappointment than from bitterness – let them serve as a moral condemnation of those who betrayed their oath, these Chilean soldiers – so-called Commanders in Chief like the self-appointed Admiral Merino, or that jackal Mr Mendoza, who only yesterday protested his loyalty to the government and has how appointed himself Director General of the Carabineros.

Faced with all these events, there is only one thing I can say to the workers: I shall not surrender.

History has given me a choice. I shall sacrifice my life in loyalty to my people, in the knowledge that the seeds we have planted in the noble consciousness of thousands of Chileans can never be prevented from bearing fruit.

Our enemies are strong; they can enslave the people. But neither criminal acts nor force of arms can hold back this social process. History belongs to us; it is the people that make history.

Workers of my country:

I want to thank you for the loyalty you have always shown, for the trust you have always placed in a man who has been no more than the interpreter of your great desire for justice, a man who undertook publicly to respect the constitution and the law and who did not betray that undertaking. This is the last chance I shall have to speak to you, to explain to you what has happened. Foreign capital and imperialism have allied with the forces of reaction to produce a climate in which the armed forces have broken with tradition. General Schneider and Commander Araya, who upheld and reasserted that tradition, have fallen victim to those people, to that class which now hopes, through its intermediaries – the armed forces – to regain the interests and privileges it had lost.

Let me speak first to the ordinary women of our country, to the peasant woman who had faith in us, to the working woman who worked even harder, to the mother who knew that her children were our concern.

Let me speak to those members of the professions who acted in patriotic fashion, who a few days ago were still resisting the mutiny led by the professional associations, the unions of the upper class, a mutiny which they hoped would allow them to retain the privileges a few of them had enjoyed under a capitalist system.

Let me speak to the young, to those who sang and who added their joy and their enthusiasm to our struggle.

Let me speak to the workers, peasants and intellectuals of Chile who will now suffer persecution, for Fascism has existed in our country for some time, and has already revealed itself in terrorism, in the sabotage of bridges, railway lines and oil pipelines.

No doubt Radio Magallanes will be silenced very soon too, and my words will no longer reach you. Yet you will continue to hear them; I shall always be with you. And at the very least I shall leave behind the memory of an honourable man, who kept faith with the working class.

The people must defend themselves; but they must avoid needless sacrifice. The people must never be crushed, humiliated or destroyed.

Workers of my country:

I have faith in Chile and in its destiny. Other Chileans will come forward. In these dark and bitter days, when treachery seeks to impose its own order, you may be assured that much sooner than later, the great avenues toward a new society will open again, and the march along that road will continue.

Long live Chile!

Long live the people!

Long live the workers!

These are my last words. I know my sacrifice has not been in vain. May it be a lesson for all those who hate disloyalty, cowardice and treachery.

Late that morning Pinochet gave the order to Carvajal, 'Now, attack the Moneda. Give it to them!'

At noon British-made warplanes moved in to bomb the Moneda palace. Allende had ordered all civilians to leave. He remained with some of his ministers and Augusto Olivares, Allende's friend and press adviser, who was killed some time before 2pm. For a time Pinochet entertained the thought that the President could be captured alive. On the radio to Carvajal he wondered about flying them away somewhere,

'Ask Leigh. My view is that these gentlemen are taken and sent anywhere. Finally on the way you throw them out.'

Allende escaped the fate which others were to suffer, of being thrown out of a plane. Some time between two and two-thirty he died, perhaps by his own hand, as troops under General Javier Palacios stormed the blazing Moneda.

Champagne and death in Santiago
Hugh O'Shaughnessy, Santiago 15 September 1973

After the bloodletting of the past few days grief-stricken mourners and exultant victors are emerging from a nightmare to bury their dead in a city that is still tense, bristling with troops, tanks and field guns and helicopters.

In the scramble for food from the few shops that are open when the curfew is lifted, no one has set his mind to unravelling the enormous implications for Chile and indeed the world, in the bloody overthrow by the military on Tuesday of Salvador Allende, the world's first freely-elected Marxist Head of State.

In a ceaseless campaign on the Catholic university television, the military are putting over the message that they did what they did for the best of reasons, that Allende was breaking up the country, that he had too many arms for his personal bodyguard, owned a lot of suits and ties, and liked Chivas Regal whisky. He also, they claim, shot himself. They intersperse their message with Fred Astaire and Mickey Mouse films, 'The Last of the Mohicans' and comments on how Indonesia is successfully attracting foreign investment.

In the middle-class districts of the city Chilean flags fly outside many houses as a sign of welcome for the military who have saved the country from a fate worse than death. In the lorry park the hauliers whose strike was the principal weapon against Allende put their vehicles in running order again and drive away giving the V sign.

In the working-class sectors, those who pinned their hopes on Allende are due to bury their dead and seek their missing sons and daughters, fearing the while that the traitor's whisper may mean death for them.

They have no reason to believe the story of Allende's suicide and prefer the reports that 'Curly', alias 'White Whiskers', died with a helmet on and a machine-gun in his hand.

In the Mexican Embassy today Doña Hortensia, his widow, and two of her daughters and some grandchildren ponder the offer of asylum in Mexico. On Wednesday five members of the family saw the coffin close for the last time on the swathed head of Allende before he was committed to the family grave in Valparaiso.

Chileans will soon have to start thinking about what to do in a country whose divisions run as deep as any in wretched Ulster. There can, of course, be no feasible doubts that the country is split.

In the second basement of the Carrera Hotel, which is still run by that well-known US business institution ITT – the International Telephone and Telegraph Corporation – the international jet set looked a bit plebeian on Tuesday in the unfamiliar setting of an air raid shelter.

The armed forces were about to launch a final assault on the Moneda Palace, 50 yards away, so the guests were crammed down to where no self-respecting American Express card owner had ever penetrated before, the 150 feet of dusty cellar between the laundry and the carpenter's shop. Nevertheless the guests managed a cheer when the radio announced that the last attack was being mounted on Allende and his government.

Up the road at the Hotel Crillón they drank champagne. The Crillón has always been thought of as a better class of place.

On Wednesday night when most of the 213 guests of the Carrera were grouped round a television set in the semi-darkness of the steel-shuttered hall they cheered again when the armed forces network ran a replay of the speech in which Air Force General Gustavo Leigh, who seems to be the toughest of the four-man Junta, announced how the Government was to extirpate the 'cancer of Marxism to the last consequences'. The cooks and cleaners grouped tightly round the service door, impassive and silent. Many were on the losing side and many doubtless were Marxists.

Yesterday afternoon the same look of impassivity and the same silence were to be seen in the streets of Santiago. At Lo Hermida, a matchwood slum whose principal amenity is the best view of the Andes in the whole of Santiago, I saw busloads of soldiers and carabineros backed by armoured cars carrying out a search to winkle out the 'new extremists' whose 'suicidal actions' the Government has been condemning so strongly since Tuesday. The same 'extremists' were presumably responsible for the furious machine-gun battles, rifle fire and explosions that I heard from the hotel during curfew last night.

The same passivity and silence was to be seen as the strollers bunched together near the Plaza de Italia to watch a carabinero bus back up against a grocer's shop and, heavily guarded by men with guns covering all angles, wait for its load of 'extremists'.

I myself was pretty silent and impassive on Thursday as I saw a macabre convoy of buses and cars led by an empty hearse take a consignment of people under heavy guard along the Avenida Providencia towards the centre of town.

The atmosphere in Santiago today is not that of Spain in 1936 with convoys of men going off shouting to the front. What remaining resistance there is to the right-wing Catholic, free-enterprise, Marxist-hating generals come from the sniper in the night. How organised the remaining resisters are is problematical.

Last night General Carlos Prats, whose departure from the Allende Government last month was the breaking of the last great dike against the tide of military opposition which swept forward to Tuesday's coup, announced on television that he had had no part in any resistance movement as had been rumoured abroad. Indeed, he said he had been seeking the necessary permission since Monday, first of the Congress while it was still alive, and now of the military Junta, to leave the country. He said he had no desire as a Christian and a soldier to have any part in the present events, so as not to add to the bloodshed of fellow countrymen. Prats crossed into Argentina today.

The Junta claims that the situation is under control throughout Chile. But sitting as I do in curfew-ridden Santiago with so far no possibility of visiting Concepción, the capital of the South which had a name for being a bastion of the left, I cannot give any independent confirmation of this claim. Nor, by the same token can I confirm the leading reports of anti-Junta activity which continue to sweep this capital. But the official radio has already revealed that 'extremists' had managed to seize some army and carabinero uniforms so troops were having to wear distinctive armbands, often bearing an official stamp.

Nor is it possible to make any coherent assessment of the number of Chileans who have died in the last few days. One can only speculate from what one has seen at first hand. I saw the bombing of the Moneda, the tank bombardment and the furious gun battles in the streets of Santiago this week. I saw men falling to the ground and being taken away in ambulances. I was in the British Embassy in the centre of the fighting when it was shot at on Tuesday as the rooftop snipers two floors above us were strafed by helicopters.

I have talked to eye-witnesses of the strafing of the Vicuña MacKenna industrial slum, of the battle for Quimantú, the Marxist publishing house which had Régis Debray on its staff and of the shooting of a dozen 'extremists' in the streets.

> Cardinal Raúl Silva Henríquez, Archbishop of Santiago, and the four bishops of Valdivia, Temuco, Los Angeles and Ancud, who form the permanent committee of the Chilean hierarchy issued a solemn statement that referred to 'the blood which has reddened our streets, our housing estates and our factories'.
>
> They were, it would seem, referring to bloodletting on a massive scale. Their statement was censored out of the Government's television programme. I have had reliable reports of many dead at the eastern campus of the Catholic University and at the Technical University where 600 students were officially reported to have been taken prisoner.
>
> On Thursday I visited the hospital of the Catholic University where I was told they had had no call to take in wounded cases and were attending only to their usual crop of ailments. I later learnt that the Posta Central, Santiago's principal hospital, had beds free.
>
> On the basis of these facts the super-optimists would conclude that there were not as many injured as thought, while it might with conviction be argued that the leaders of the coup are sticking to their ultimatum of three o'clock on Tuesday afternoon to the effect that all resisters captured would be shot.
>
> Whether 1,000, 5,000, 10,000 or 15,000 died in Chile this week, one cannot but fear for the future of this bloodstained land.
>
> *The Observer*, 16 September 1973

At four o'clock on that fine spring day at the Military School Pinochet, Leigh, Merino and Mendoza sealed their treachery by appointing themselves as a military junta with unlimited powers, closing Congress and forbidding party political activity. They then turned their attention to the 'enemy'.

Pinochet chose one of his closest colleagues to oversee the onslaught against the left. As a retired army colonel, Olagier Benavente was to reveal in an interview conducted in June 1999 that the general's personal pilot, Captain Antonio Palomo, a favourite of Pinochet's and who had been entrusted with several delicate jobs at home and abroad for the newly installed dictator, was given a special task.

Helicopters were put at his disposal at the army air corps headquarters at the airfield at Tobalaba on the outskirts of the capital and he was told to load up a number of political prisoners, and, it appears, some corpses of prisoners. Those who were put in the 'Puerto

62

Montt' category were tossed out in the high Andes; those in the 'Moneda' category were dumped in the Pacific. Asked whether those dumped at sea had a weight round their necks or had their chests opened so they would not float, Benavente's reply was impassive: 'I suppose that they threw them out with some stone.' Palomo became commander of the army air corps in 1983 and Pinochet rewarded him three years later with a posting to the Chilean embassy in Paris as a military attaché.

Benavente, seventy years old at the time of his statement, balding a little but keeping a well-trimmed white moustache, had been one of the first to act against the opponents of the new regime. He was made governor of the city of Talca and on the very day of the coup presided over a military tribunal which condemned to death Germán Castro, a 33 year-old accountant who was the city's mayor. 'We shot him at midnight at the barracks, then we put him in the morgue at the cemetery and buried him the next day,' he explained.

General Arellano, the acknowledged leader of the plotting against Allende well before Pinochet joined the conspiracy, was ordered to fly round the country in October to 'inspect the system of military justice'. The result of was that more than seventy people in custody in various provincial cities were summarily murdered in what became known as 'the Caravan of Death'.

On 15 September, four days after the coup and two months after Lucía and Augusto's kind note to their friends the Tohás, José Tohá was sent by Pinochet, along with many others of Allende's immediate circle such as Orlando Letelier, Allende's former ambassador to Washington and foreign minister, to the remote and inhospitable Dawson Island in the Magellan Straits. After being made to work in the mud, driving rain and cold, Tohá fell ill. He was brought back to Santiago for medical treatment in February 1974 and died on 15 March. The official version said that he hanged himself by a belt in his room at the military hospital.

Another case was that of air force general Alberto Bachelet. Three days before his death Bachelet was taken to the War Academy, where he underwent interrogation, having been tortured by his former subordinates. He was then kept prisoner in the public jail. While he was washing plates in the jail kitchen he began to feel ill. He died in the company of his fellow prisoners on 12 March 1974.

The DINA

General Augusto Pinochet's first use of overwhelming force to propel him and his comrades-in-arms into full control of the country was followed by the formulation of a medium-term strategy which would destroy any challenge to his own rule from inside or outside the country.

His strategy was to a large extent planned by his former pupil Colonel Manuel Contreras Sepúlveda, known to his intimates as 'Mamo'. Apart from his wife and his mother Contreras was to be the person who had the most influence on Pinochet.

They had first got to know each other when Pinochet was a captain teaching in the Military School. Contreras, an engineer by training, showed a particular interest in Pinochet's subjects of geopolitics and intelligence and was the best student of his year. Pinochet was to be the godfather to one of Contreras' children.

In 1967 Contreras, by now a major, underwent two years of training with the US Army at Fort Belvoir in Virginia, where he would have come into contact with US Cold War attitudes. Politically, Contreras would become an energetic advocate of a political doctrine of totalitarianism. (He found a fellow spirit in Pinochet's wife, whose indignation with those who crossed her husband was, and continues to be, great. In 1984 she was to declare, 'If I was head of government I'd be much harder than my husband. I'd have the whole of Chile under a state of siege.' She acknowledged that some of her anger at the time was the result of the sabotage of electric power lines then being carried out by opponents of the regime. 'There are power cuts now. Without power', she pointed out, in an interesting show of priorities, 'shops and hairdressing salons can't function!')

Pinochet relied more on Contreras than on any other officer. Because of his privileged position as an intimate of the General, Contreras inevitably came into conflict with other officers, including his superior officers in the army. There was also friction with the navy and air force who were keen not to surrender their influence to the army and to Pinochet. Contreras also made enemies among the civilians who wanted Chile to move rapidly to a regime of modern capitalism. Nevertheless he battled on, basking in the favour of the most powerful man in the country.

With the coup, Pinochet and his co-conspirators had undoubtedly stolen the initiative. There was no real organised resistance to the new regime in Chile. At home, the Junta had less to worry about from its political enemies than from opponents and rivals within the armed forces in particular the army. Similarly, outside the country the danger to his position came less from foreign enemies than from Chileans who might set up a government-in-exile.

In any case, foreign governments and international public opinion were soon distracted from a military coup in South America to the latest round of hostilities between Arabs and Israelis in the Middle East. By 1974 the OPEC oil crisis had pushed Chile and Pinochet off the front pages of world newspapers.

The instrument chosen to deal with rivals within the armed forces and the exile community was the Directorate of National Intelligence, the DINA. The organisation was formally established on June 14, 1974 though its origins went back to at least November of the previous year or even before. Pinochet chose Contreras as its director.

The DINA logo was a fist wearing a gauntlet. The letterhead proclaimed simply:

Republic of Chile
Presidency of the Republic
DINA

Anyone receiving a message on paper with such a heading knew they were in direct touch with Augusto Pinochet Ugarte. Following his 1998 arrest in Britain, Pinochet's supporters put forward the defence that Pinochet never knew of the human rights abuses committed by the DINA under Contreras. But in a testimony to the Chilean Supreme Court in 1998, Contreras, now a general on the retired list, stated that he had been named to head the DINA on the verbal order of Pinochet.

He had never had a formal, written appointment and, he added, 'I only served as the delegate of the President', reporting to him directly, 'without any intermediary'. His orders always came, Contreras insisted, from Pinochet himself.

The DINA was established as independent of the intelligence services of the army, navy, air force and carabineros. It was ruthless and cordially hated by Pinochet's enemies and some of his allies. But as an intelligence and terror agency it was also bold and efficient, acting as Pinochet's eyes and ears. It was common for Contreras to have breakfast with Pinochet almost daily and thereafter ride in his car to the Junta's headquarters in the Edificio Diego Portales. In his sworn testimony to the Chilean Supreme Court in 1998 Contreras said that the DINA had been a military body which at first depended directly on the President of the Junta, Pinochet, and later, on the President of the Republic, also Pinochet, and that it never had the authority to take decisions of its own accord.

The DINA's ranks were made up of army and carabinero officers, with the occasional participation of navy and air force personnel. A foreign department was formally set up in April 1974 and this recruited civilian staff from nationalist and extreme right-wing political groups. Several of the DINA's most notorious agents who would go on to carry out assassinations and assassination attempts abroad came from essentially a civilian background.

The DINA also controlled detention and torture centres and clinics through the country. One torture centre was next door to the British Council, with its classrooms for teaching English principally to middle-class youngsters and its quiet reading room where *The Daily Telegraph* and *The Economist* were available. Another, a few blocks away was at 38 Calle Londres. The biggest DINA centre was the Villa Grimaldi in the La Reina quarter of the city; Tejas Verdes was part of a military base housing the School of Military Engineering not far from the capital; the London Clinic was a little farther away in the Calle Almirante Barroso; Cuatro Alamos was a torture centre in Vicuña Mackenna, a main avenue in the capital; the Discoteca or Venda Sexy which became particularly known for sexual atrocities was at 3037 Calle Irán in the Quilín quarter of the city and was so-named because music was constantly audible from it.

There were many centres outside the capital, the most notorious being the Colonia Dignidad, a large estate near Parral in the south of the country. Colonia Dignidad was the hideout of a secretive group of Germans who faced charges of paedophilia in Germany but who had successfully resisted intrusion and extradition under Christian Democratic, Socialist and military regimes for decades.

Some details of the torture regime were contained in the Rettig Report. Others, involving children and minors, were set out in unadorned form in the charges laid by the Crown Prosecution Service on behalf of the Kingdom of Spain against Pinochet in the sober surroundings of a British court.

One of the charges alleged that he, 'being a public official, namely the Commander in Chief of the Chilean Army' did intentionally inflict:

severe pain or suffering on Pedro Hugo Arellano Carvajal by:

- tying him to a metal bed and forcing his hands against an electrified metal plate, throwing him across the room from the shock;

- electrocuting him with electric wires attached to his chest, his penis and his toes;

- trying him to a tree and whipping him;

- placing him on board a helicopter, pushing him out with ropes tied to his trousers, and dragging him through thorns:

- tying him to a rope and lowering him into a well, until he was nearly drowned, pulling him out, and lowering him back into the well when he failed to answer questions;

- subjecting him to 'Russian roulette';

- forcing him to take all his clothes off in the presence of the captive Rodriguez family who had been arrested with their sons, forcing him to witness torture of that family as the father was made to bugger his son, as, simultaneously, that son was made to bugger his younger brother;

- forcing him to bugger one of those sons himself;

in purported performance of official duties.

Dozens more charges like that were laid against the man who professed his devotion to Christianity in general and to the Virgin of Mount Carmel in particular.

Diary of a Chilean Concentration Camp

My jaws are quivering, I don't know what to say, I can't think what to invent. Open-mouthed, I toss my head from side to side, nothing comes out. Then they stick something over my tongue and a hand's clamped over my mouth. The discharge rocks my tongue and penis simultaneously. I wrench my shoulders out of joint with the contractions. I don't lose consciousness. The pain approximates, on the one hand, to a mutilation. It's as if they'd torn my penis up by the roots, like something taking a giant bite out of me, and then, in my mouth, like an explosion blasting away the flesh, laying bare the bones of my face and neck, leaving the nerves petrified, in a vacuum. Even more than that, there's no recollection of the pain.

'Did he proposed taking action against the Junta?'

I move my head up and down, lots of times, rapidly. Yes, he proposed whatever they want him to have proposed. I get another discharge, less violent.

'Who was party to the decision?'

The hand removes itself from my mouth. My tongue's rigid, the skin of the roof of my mouth shrivelled, dry like a nutshell. I barely hear what I say, hoarsely. I give a few names and, in my concern to leave someone out, name someone else who wasn't there.

'And he said he was collaborating in the international Marxist campaign against Chile?'

Yes, of course, whatever they want.

'And to think you made all that fuss over a little thing like that, you son of a bitch!'

They give me a last, farewell discharge in the penis. They untie me.

'Get dressed, you fucking queer.'

I slide off the stretched and grope all around the floor. I can't remember where I got undressed.

'Hurry up, you shit.'

They kick me in the right direction. There's no time for the pain to register. I get the clothes all jumbled up, I can't find the trouserlegs.

'Put your pants on first, you shit! Get yourself dressed properly.'

Hernán Valdés, *Diary of a Chilean Concentration Camp*

Pinochet relied on the DINA to keep him informed of the thinking within the armed forces and the carabineros. In the first instance he had to crush opposition within the armed forces themselves. The Rettig report lists 132 members of the armed forces, the carabineros and Investigaciones, the criminal investigation department, as having been murdered during the Pinochet years, with the carabineros suffering the largest number of casualties – 69.

A difficult thorn in Pinochet's side was General Oscar Bonilla, who at the time of the coup was sixth in seniority in the army. Bonilla was close to the Christian Democrat Party and seemed to have ambitions to take over the command of the army after what most Chileans expected would be a short period of military rule. In the first cabinet formed after the coup, Bonilla, an enthusiastic plotter against Allende, was named interior minister.

On 10 April 1974, Pinochet announced a cull of Generals Orlando Urbina, Rolando Torres, Manuel Torres and Ernesto Baeza. Bonilla moved up to second in seniority in the army behind Pinochet himself. In July 1974, just after the electoral registers were incinerated, he was given the job of defence minister. He became one of the first military men to feel the strain inside a regime which Pinochet was determined to control for his own interests. Bonilla's dilemma was compounded by Pinochet's close contact with Contreras, who, as a colonel and lower ranking officer, was supposed to answer directly to Bonilla. As interior minister, Bonilla soon became one of the many senior officers infuriated with Pinochet's relationship with Contreras.

Bonilla had to personally field a growing number of pleas on behalf of the regime's – or, more correctly, DINA's – victims, with an increasing number of petitioners arriving at his house. He helped with legal connections, but he must have felt frustrated that he could do no more.

His anger was no doubt shared by many generals. At one cabinet meeting Contreras' arrogance provoked a confrontation. Contreras called for increased watchfulness in the ministries, as some documents had been stolen. According to Ascanio Cavallo, a journalist and historian of the Pinochet years, the colonel said that the theft had been the result of left-wing infiltration. Bonilla exploded, 'Colonel, what proof have you got for what you're saying?' Looking at Pinochet, Contreras replied, 'General, there are certain things which cannot be talked about in front of outsiders.' Bonilla, it appears, was ready to hit him but Pinochet quickly changed the subject.

A few months later General Bonilla attempted to get his own back on the colonel when he presented the file on one particular victim, a businessman who had been tortured and managed to escape and a few days later saw his son kidnapped in a fit of DINA vengeance. Bonilla made a formal move for the sacking of Contreras. He got an evasive reply; the case would be studied.

Meanwhile Brigadier-General Augusto Lutz, director of army intelligence and a devout Catholic who had opposed the army take-over of the Catholic University, also stepped into the ring with Contreras. General Lutz, who had had training at the US School of the Americas, brought up the case of the kidnapping of the husband of a teacher at his son's school. The general phoned the colonel and asked for the details of the case. Contreras replied simply, 'You don't have access to that information, general. Only the President.'

Lutz blew up. 'Who do you think you are! How dare you talk like that to a general of the republic like that! You'll see!'

Brigadier-General Sergio Arellano, the commander of the Santiago garrison, one of the 1973 plotters and just superior in seniority to Lutz, wrote a personal letter to Pinochet pointing to the arbitrary nature of the terror and how Colonel Contreras would give him no information. He said, 'People are talking of a real Gestapo'.

General Lutz was soon eased out of his post at the head of military intelligence and sent off to command the V Division based at Punta Arenas in the remote south of the country. He knew his time with Pinochet was running out and confessed to his family in 1974 that he would be leaving the army that year. 'I can't take any more', he commented.

After a cocktail party in Punta Arenas, the general, a non-drinker, was taken ill and was admitted to the town's hospital where the diagnosis was of varicose veins in his oesophagus, an affliction more common in drinkers. He was operated on, but blood poisoning set in and the diagnosis was seen to have been inaccurate. On 8 November he was flown back to Santiago, where a helicopter took him to the military hospital. There, surrounded by a guard commanded by a colonel and with all visitors but his wife barred from his bed, the general underwent a series of operations. As he

70

lay there he found strength to compose one faintly written message, '*Sáquenme de aquí.*' (Get me out of here). The family put it down to delirium. On 28 November 1974 he died of blood poisoning.

Given the quantity of errors that had been committed in the case an enquiry was opened and the family was called to give evidence. Early in 1975 his widow returned to the doctor who had been given the task of investigating the circumstances of Lutz's death to find out what the results of the enquiry were. 'What enquiry?' asked the doctor.

For Pinochet there remained the problem of General Bonilla. The defence minister had been formally designated by Pinochet as his successor at the head of the army. On the misty morning of 3 March 1975 General Bonilla took a U-H1H helicopter at El Calabozo, near the southern town of Romeral. He boarded and the rotors whirred. It appeared that he had misgivings about the flight. He alighted and banged on the pilot's door shouting, 'Are you sure we can fly?' 'Yes, general, don't worry,' came the reply. It was a bumpy ride and at one point a captain and a major in the cockpit were fighting over the controls while General Bonilla shouted, 'What's going on?' from the back seat. The helicopter crashed in a field soon after, killing Bonilla and everyone else on board.

Within hours French technicians and the air force were on the scene. All were puzzled that the tail rotor had fallen so far away from the site of the crash. The investigation was taken over by the army; an air force corporal involved in the original investigation was sent off to France to re-take a course he had already taken; the French experts were injured in another helicopter crash, and the findings of the enquiry into that accident were marked secret. The authorities let it be known that General Bonilla had insisted on taking off at any cost.

The Church

'At the end of that terrible month even my house was searched. A group of soldiers from the air force searched it all over arguing that a plastic object had fallen from an aircraft in that area and they needed to get it back. Of course the blessed object was not there.'
    Cardinal Raúl Silva, *Memoirs*, writing of September 1973.

In the first years of his regime Pinochet faced serious opposition from the Catholic church. This opposition arose not so much from the Chilean clergy's dislike of the country's new leader – many of them heartily approved of the new order. Rather was it sustained by the formidable personality of Cardinal Raúl Silva Henríquez, Archbishop of Santiago. Silva was an outstanding example of the best of the Roman Catholic episcopate in Latin America, a man of humility, active on behalf of the poor and for human rights.

Raúl Silva was born the sixteenth of nineteen children of an impoverished family in the southern city of Talca. He rose rapidly in the church and John XXIII named him Bishop of Valparaiso in 1959. He was appointed Archbishop of Santiago in 1961, becoming cardinal the following year. He had had a good relationship with the Christian Democratic government of President Frei Montalva and thereafter, more surprisingly, with Allende. Allende had said to him, 'I can promise you, Don Raúl, that I won't touch the Church, not even with a rose petal.' Though there were tensions with Allende, notably about reform of education, they were overcome. 'He was always prepared to talk and find a solution', said the cardinal in 1983. During the Allende years Silva's refusal to manoeuvre against the elected government alienated him from many rich Chileans. As far as Pinochet was concerned Silva was, as Margaret Thatcher might have put it, 'not one of us'.

Silva, along with many other Chileans, suffered a rude awakening when the military plotters staged their September 1973 putsch. He was upset when an emissary from Pinochet arrived at his house a few days after the coup, accompanied by an army chaplain in uniform and carrying a pistol.

'What on earth are you doing with that pistol in your belt, hombre?' the cardinal asked the priest.

'Your Eminence, these are dangerous times.'

'But you're a priest!'

'I'm a military chaplain, Your Eminence.'

'And what does that mean? Are you going to shoot with that thing? Are you going to kill somebody?'

About the same time Silva vetoed Pinochet's wish to have a Te Deum for the new regime celebrated in the Military School. (It was eventually held in a place of worship in the capital whose full title was 'The Church of National Gratitude to the Sacred Heart of Jesus for the Triumph of Arms and Heroes of the War of the Pacific'.) Guided by Silva, the bishops' conference angered Pinochet, too, by its refusal to refer to the coup as a patriotic act of national salvation.

Within a few days of the coup priests were being killed. The Anglo-Chilean Michael Woodward died under torture aboard the warship *Lebu* in Valparaiso harbour. Joan Alsina, a Spaniard, was interrogated by the navy and his body was fished out of the River Mapocho in Santiago a few days later with thirteen bullet holes in his back.

On 1 October another Spanish priest, Antonio Llidó, was arrested. He was seen in two torture centres in the capital but disappeared at the end of the month. In Iquique Gerardo Poblete, a member of the cardinal's own Salesian order and a schoolteacher, was arrested on 25 October. The army said he had slipped from a truck while handcuffed, banged his head and was later found unconscious in his cell. 'The cause of death was his fall from truck No. 693,' it concluded.

Even the least concerned diocesan bishops are usually upset when their staff are murdered. Tyrants have been excommunicated for less than Pinochet was responsible for. All, however, was not lost for Pinochet. He had a useful potential ally in Raúl Hasbún, a priest on Silva's staff who had been a fierce propagandist against Allende. Hasbún fought against the military take-over of the Catholic University, where he was a director of the television station Channel 13. He had to be sacked by the rector, Admiral Jorge Swett, but the government knew he had no love for the supporters of Allende.

Three weeks after the coup Bishop Alfredo Cifuentes of La Serena made a special donation to the authorities. 'With deep patriotic emotion', he said, 'I have the honour of putting in the hands of the Honourable Junta my pastoral ring so as to make a modest contribution to the work of Chile's reconstruction.' A few weeks later Bishop Eladio Vicuña of Chillán said in reference to the abolition of democracy and the Congress, 'It's a great benefit to the country that the Honourable Governing Junta has imposed political silence for a long period.'

Cardinal Raúl Silva had his feet planted more firmly on the ground. The first statement of the bishops conference enraged the Junta by its coolness to the coup and its refusal to refer to it as a patriotic act of national salvation. Within a month of the coup the Cardinal moved quickly to create an ecumenical human rights organisation to aid the victims of the military. The Comité Pro Paz was presided over by a Catholic bishop its leaders included those of the Jewish community, Baptists, Methodists, Pentecostal Methodists, Lutherans and Orthodox and a representative of the World Council of Churches.

Within a month, too, Rome, fully advised of the desperate situation in Chile, was ready to move. Pope Paul VI wrote a confidential letter to the Chilean bishops expressing his horror at the killings and his desire for democracy to be restored and announcing publicly in Rome his pain at the Junta's 'bloody repression'. The nunciature, whose secretary at that time was Mgr Piero Biggio, later himself nuncio in Santiago, was unhappy with the letter. The nuncio, Mgr Sótero Sanz, begged Silva to dissuade the Pope from publishing it and thus severely embarrassing Pinochet. On 3 November the cardinal went on a flying visit to Rome and did exactly that, an action which he was later to bitterly regret.

Meanwhile, the Junta did their best to have the 'subversive' Silva removed from the primacy of Chile. With the help of Franco supporters among the Spanish bishops, efforts were made to have Silva promoted to a post in Rome. At the same time the regime made attempts to discredit him by linking him to supposed financial irregularities in a small vineyard he owned. Soon the Pope issued a discreet investigation, noted that this cleared him of any financial wrongdoing and gave him increased Vatican funds for his charitable works. The cardinal's Comité Pro Paz continued its work as one of the very few friends of those Chileans undergoing persecution or torture.

The persecution, harassment and torture of clerics continued on a large scale for many years more. For instance, on 30 November

1975 Pinochet's secret police shot their way into the house of the Columban Fathers in the Chilean capital, killing a housekeeper at the door.

Silva went on another visit to Pope Paul in Rome. The cardinal begged the Pope to publish the letter that he had persuaded the Pope not to publish two years previously. The Pope is reported to have said, 'No, Raúl, the moment's gone. You've lost your opportunity.' The Pope did however tell Cardinal Silva to inform General Pinochet that he considered those Chilean priests who were being persecuted as 'martyrs of Christian charity.'

The Comité Pro Paz was forcibly dissolved by the regime on 27 November 1975. Undaunted, in 1976 Silva founded a new body, the Vicariate of Solidarity (the *Vicaría*) , a purely catholic body, answerable to him, to assist the persecuted.

In March 1977 the bishops' conference issued a document in which they demanded that 'the fate of each one of those presumed to have disappeared since 11 September to date be clarified once and for all.' Until that happened, it added, 'there will be no peace for their relatives, nor real peace in the country and the image of Chile will not be clean abroad.'

In March 1977 Miguel Schweitzer was replaced as justice minister by Renato Damilano, a schoolfriend of Pinochet's schooldays in Valparaiso. It was not a clever choice. Within days of his installation the new minister decided to launch an out-and-out attack on the church at a university lecture. He lashed out at senior clergy, who 'abandoning the care of souls and forgetting that 'my kingdom is not of this world' throw themselves into a hypocritical political campaign against the government. They talk in the name of charity and, as they do, sin against charity. Thus do labour the worshippers of Marx and Lenin, with the enthusiastic collaboration of the useful idiots, of the ambitious, of the ill-intentioned, of the resentful and of those who abandon their sacred ministry to take the place vacated by those parties which, in one form or other, contributed to the destruction of the country.'

The bishops immediately protested in the strongest terms and Pinochet was forced to say that Damilano had been speaking personally. But the minister went on to stand by what he had said in an interview with a Santiago newspaper. Within six weeks he was removed from the post.

Silva's Vicariate's work was recognised when the UN decided to give it its human rights award in a ceremony in New York in 1978, an event which marked a watershed for Pinochet's relations with the church. That year Pope Paul died and his two successors, John Paul I whose reign lasted a month and the Polish John Paul II were named in quick succession.

In the nunciature in Santiago there were similar changes. Monsignor Angelo Sodano, whose experience of Chile dated back to the last days of the Allende government and the first days of the military dictatorship, returned as head of the nunciature. Silva at the same time was entering the twilight of his episcopate, as he approached the age of 75 when he was expected to tender his resignation. Pinochet began to breathe more freely about his relations with one of the most powerful of Chile's institutions.

Meanwhile Pinochet had escaped formal and personal excommunication, the ultimate sanction of the Catholic Church. Excommunication would have caused him great personal difficulties and might even have put a rapid end to a dictator who was constantly declaring his devotion to the defence of 'Western Christian civilisation'.

He avoided the censure by a hair's breadth. Silva had been mulling over the idea of excommunicating him. The cardinal was later to make a dreadful avowal to his close collaborator Hernán Montealegre, Chile's most prominent human rights lawyer. In some anguish Silva told Montealegre that there was one particular omission that he would have to answer to God for: he had never formally expelled the General from the church.

In December 1980 seven bishops from six sees, Talca, Linares, Valdivia, Ancud, Temuco and Punta Arenas, issued decrees of excommunication against all those who participated in torture, incited, ordered or solicited it, or, being in a position to halt it, did not do so. Three years later the bishops' conference adopted the decree of the seven sees, ruling in an agreed document that 'torturers, their accomplices, and those who are able to stop torture and do not do it, cannot receive Holy Communion nor can they morally be godparents in the Sacraments of the Church, unless they sincerely repent.'

Though Pinochet was never excommunicated by name, many in Chile believe that his active promotion of torture and his unwillingness to abjure it means de facto that he cannot any longer a member of the church. He himself was perhaps thinking of this position when he declared in June 1984, 'I pray with the frequency that a good catholic should. In the morning, in the afternoon and at night. But I have distanced myself a little from some activities'.

That he was excommunicated is certainly the opinion of Bishop Carlos González of Punta Arenas. In his book *Torture of Eucharist*, Dr William T. Cavanaugh of the University of St Thomas in St Paul, Minnesota, recounts a conversation with Bishop González who in reply to the question of whether Pinochet had been excommunicated said, 'He is excommunicated. Yes, yes. If he gave orders to torture, you saw the decree. If Pinochet is the intellectual author, he is excommunicated. If he is not, he is not excommunicated.'

In September 1982, on his 75th birthday, Silva flew to Rome and tendered his resignation which the Pope accepted with alacrity. Pinochet's diplomats had maintained a constant drip of complaint to Rome against Silva, blaming him for anything that they disliked inside or outside his archdiocese. The resignation was announced in May 1983. Pinochet's wife Lucía exclaimed, 'It seems God has heard us.'

Pinochet's position with the Catholic Church demonstrated the serious clash of interests between the local Christian community and the worldwide interests of the Vatican.

On the one hand there were bishops like Silva, trying to protect his people from the worst actions of a military regime, and on the other, Vatican diplomats like Sodano, charged with maintaining the Holy See's relations with that same regime.

Nuncio Sodano cultivated strong relations with the Chilean right and with Pinochet himself. The general must have been grateful for the relationship he had forged with Sodano years later when the latter was appointed Vatican Secretary of State. At the end of 1998 Sodano tried to intercede with the British Government and with the Archbishop of Canterbury for Pinochet's immediate release from custody on 'humanitarian grounds'.

Meanwhile, in February 1999 Archbishop Francisco Javier Errázuriz of Santiago said that the treatment meted out to the General in London meant that British justice was defective and the British themselves uncivilised. Errázuriz had already been quoted in the 24 October 1998 edition of pro-Pinochet daily *El Mercurio* as saying of the arrest of Pinochet was a barbarity. The archbishop of Santiago declared, 'I've asked the lawyers who so defend human rights in Chile if at any time under the military government there had been a similar situation with a person of that age. They said no.'

King Emperor

'I've got a sour face, perhaps that's why they say I'm a dictator.'
Augusto Pinochet, August 1986

On 27 June 1974 Pinochet formally assumed the title of Supreme Chief of the Nation. He had outflanked his three fellow members of the Junta – something that no one, possibly even Pinochet, could have foreseen, although he did command the most powerful of the four armed forces.

The navy was out of the race for supremacy through the simple fact that no force of sailors could ever take control of any inland part of Chile against the will of the army. Moreover its leader, Admiral José Toribio Merino, was not a forceful character. The commander of the carabineros, Chile's armed police (familarly known as the *pacos*), could for his part never aspire to the top job. After all, where had the strong man ever worn a policeman's uniform in Latin America, apart from Uruguay for a brief period in the 1930s?

There remained one problem. General Gustavo Leigh Guzmán, commander-in-chief of the air force and a fellow member of the Junta, was not willing to admit or publicly acknowledge Pinochet's paramountcy. Worse, Leigh was pressing for a wholesale transformation of the system of government Pinochet had striven so hard to establish.

Leigh had harboured resentment since the first days of the coup. In terms of military protocol he was the senior of the four members of the Junta, and from his own point of view the most legitimate member. He had a case that he should be Chief of the Junta as he had been appointed to head the air force by Allende on 20 August three days before the President made Pinochet commander-in-chief of the army.

Seniority, always a tricky subject in the military world, was a particularly thorny issue in a group where personal rivalries were strong. It was a headache for the aides-de-camp on formal occasions to find doors wide enough to allow their four chiefs to enter walking four abreast.

At the beginning Pinochet was formally no more than *primus inter pares*. It had been eventually agreed among the four that seniority should be measured by the seniority of the service and not of the man in command. The army took precedence as the oldest established armed force, followed by the navy, the air force and the carabineros.

But Leigh was resentful of the fact that Pinochet tended to present the other members of the Junta with a course of action, rather than discussing the decision with him. Leigh, who had appeared the firmest and most aggressive of the four on the day of the coup, soon seemed to be veering away from the idea of a long-term dictatorship – particularly if the dictator was to be Pinochet. When Pinochet showed Leigh a draft decree creating a president, Leigh objected, citing the excessive concentration of power it entailed and the bad image it projected internationally. Infuriated, Pinochet stood up, tore the paper into little pieces, threw them in the waste paper basket and stormed out of the room.

On 17 June 1974 Pinochet had gathered his three colleagues together to present them with the text of Decree 527, which granted him seniority. The meeting ended in acrimony, but eventually it was pushed through by Pinochet.

An hour or so before the public proclamation of the decree on 27 June, the president of the Supreme Court was instructed to preside at the ceremony. The press too were alerted. Only subsequently were Pinochet's three Junta colleagues informed. Voices were raised as they realised that they would either have to assent to a public ceremony or publicly reveal to the world serious splits within the Junta.

Leigh was the most angry. He shouted to Pinochet, 'You think you're God! How much longer is this going on!' Equally forcefully Pinochet shouted back, 'That's enough fucking around! If there's so much row we'll call off the ceremony and we'll see what'll happen then! I'm not going to allow the country to be played about with!' He brought his fist down so hard on the table that the glass top shattered.

At the ensuing ceremony Pinochet merely signed a 'supreme decree', which did not need the approval of the Junta as a whole. He then began to sign documents 'by order of the President'. As a further symbol of his victory each of the four services was called on to provide him with an aide-de-camp.

Pinochet set up office in the Diego Portales building originally built for the UN Conference on Trade and Development, now taken over as the centre of government until the bombed-out Moneda Palace could be repaired. Before long he had taken over two whole floors. On the 22nd was his office, his secretariat and the large conference room. On the floor below were his auxiliary services. He demonstrated the hierarchy in vertical terms: the navy was demoted to the twentieth floor, the air force to the nineteenth and the carabineros to the eighteenth.

Pinochet had consolidated his position, officially and symbolically. At last the Junta's protocol officers could stop worrying about finding wide-doored rooms. From now on the Junta would enter with Pinochet at the head of the line.

Laughing in the face of terror

The lowly status of the carabineros and their commander General César Mendoza, as they tried to keep their end up beside the 'genuine warriors' in the army, navy and air force, was the constant butt of jokes in the city. No less a target was General Mendoza's mental acumen. One described how, towards the end of a particularly long and tiring Junta meeting, Pinochet paused and barked out, 'Mendoza, three coffees!' The Carabinero general, abashed, stammered, 'But Augusto, I'm a general and a member of the Junta like the rest of you!' Pinochet shot back, 'OK, Mendocita, four coffees!'

The Pinochet family's general lack of culture was also quietly ridiculed. The story went the rounds of how the dictator's wife left the theatre after a ballet performance gushing with pleasure. 'Knowing how tired Augusto was,' she was reported to have said, 'those dancers were so kind and considerate. They danced on tiptoe so as not to wake him up!'

Pinochet remained always acutely aware of position, and his concern for hierarchical decorum extended into the Junta's social life. During one performance of Carmen at the capital's main theatre, the Teatro Municipal, General Leigh had been given a spontaneous round of applause in the presidential box. Soon after Pinochet issued a memorandum announcing that this box would be reserved for Pinochet alone and the rest would have to sit elsewhere.

From the day of the coup until well after Pinochet quit the presidency, Chile was a society ruled by fear. To instil fear had been the objective of a policy which seized people off the street for sessions of torture and then released them to pass the word about the punishments which awaited the dictator's opponents. The press and the publishing houses which had supported the constitutional government disappeared and the rest made sure that they did not bring out anything that could upset the dictator.

A few days after the coup I met a distinguished right-wing senator in the street and asked his opinion about the future of the Junta. He assured me that parliamentary rule would be restored before many weeks were out and I included that in a dispatch to London. His forecast, however, did not get transmitted. A kindly old gentlemen with a neat white moustache, who I later learnt was a retired colonel, sat in the Transradio telex office used by the few foreign correspondents in the Chilean capital. After reading what I had written, he carefully put a blue pencil through all references I had made to the senator and then with great courtesy passed on what was left to the telex operator for transmission. News reports in Chile became useful only as an indication of the military's thinking.

The arts in Chile continued to exist only in so far as they represented classical and conservative forms, such as opera and ballet. A generation of writers, playwrights, songwriters and musicians, starting with the singer Víctor Jara, were either killed or exiled by the regime.

Numismatics was taken on as a prop to the regime with coins minted showing a female figure breaking out of chains and the legend, '*Libertad*', freedom. In the social sphere there was little of either; for example, the new regime gave no encouragement for those who were campaigning for divorce and abortion. Even today, married couples wishing to split up continue to have recourse to the polite fiction of annulment, which is easily available.

The elimination of opposition abroad

In the first years of his dictatorship Pinochet met little challenge from foreign powers. In theory, Chile was surrounded by hostile neighbours. It had strained relationships with Peru, Bolivia and Argentina, but none of Chile's immediate neighbours presented any threat to the fledgling dictatorship. Internationally, there was condemnation of the coup, but little real action.

Pinochet could have a certain confidence in the major power in the hemisphere, the United States, with President Nixon and his principal adviser Dr Henry Kissinger in power. The government-to-government relationship with the US was strengthened under the Democrats when the dictator was received by President Carter in Washington in September 1977. The US president had called together Western Hemisphere heads of state to witness the treaty which was to hand back to Panamanians the control of the Panama Canal.

The relationship between the DINA/CNI (National Information Commission) and the US intelligence services was similarly strengthened as both institutions recruited anti-Castro Cuban extremists for their operations involving violence. The Cuban exiles had been vital to the Bay of Pigs invasion and later for actions against the government of Nicaragua, while the Chilean organisation fished from the same pool of expert anti-communist personnel for their murder, narcotics and intelligence operations.

From Cuba, Fidel Castro sent a torrent of invective against Pinochet over the air waves. But though he had been supportive of Allende, the Cuban leader was cautious about the immediate future. In a fiery speech to a large crowd in Revolution Square in Havana on 28 September the Cuban leader promised Cubans would 'tear their hearts out' for Chile. He predicted a struggle would eventually lead to 'the victory of the people' but added, 'It will not be immediate. No one can expect miracles in the Chilean situation. The people have been hard hit; the parties, the organisations will have to recover from the fascist onslaught. Without any doubt the struggle of the Chilean people will have to be a long one.'

The character of treachery

The transformation from the seemingly apolitical, rather grey and hard-working Pinochet into a dictator who showed no concern for the principles of government, fair play, the law, or indeed friendship, is a startling one.

What was behind this brusque metamorphosis of a man who had received a pious education amid a loving family, who had been cherished by his grandmother, mother and his wife, who had been a loving son, husband and father of five children? This man had also been an officer respectful of his superiors and diligent to the point of workaholicism, and who gave no sign at all of departing from the recent practice of the Chilean army of being obedient to the civil power, even if that civil power was socialist.

This was the man who had had to be restrained from annihilating the mutinous armoured unit earlier in 1973 when it had the effrontery to try and stage a coup against his elected president, Salvador Allende. He had had a close lifelong relationship with his friend and comrade-in-arms Carlos Prats, the soul of respect for the constitution; he had shown no hint of been convinced by US arguments that the Cold War meant that Latin American states and their armies should accept tutelage from Washington.

He and his wife had recently had a friendly social relationship with Allende's defence minister, a socialist. He was the last senior officer but one to sign up to the plot only three days before it was enacted and had shown some hesitation when he finally did sign.

In retrospect, speculation about Pinochet's motives and character has centred on what might be called pure opportunism. It is possible that a series of factors in his character and his experience crystallised in the crucible of a day on which the history of Chile turned, a day which presented Pinochet with an unprecedented chance for almost unlimited power.

If we consider Pinochet's humble beginnings, his education alongside boys from richer families than his, the relatively low status of army officers on the Chilean social ladder, the contempt that he had suffered from his mother-in-law, the wife of a prominent politician, his early lack of money and the continual fight he had to make his modest earnings finance the demands of a family of seven, plus the possibility that he had been snubbed by the freemasons as punishment for his own lack of enthusiasm for their craft – could all this have built a head of hidden but powerful resentment which exploded into savage action on the Tuesday of the coup?

The reliable Pinochet was transformed into a being who was going to allow nothing, certainly not any vestigial twinges of conscience, to separate him from the power which he had inherited almost by accident. On various occasions he was to claim that he was guided by God. In 1974 he stated, 'Whoever analyses the military pronouncement of 1973 comes to the conclusion that the hand of God was present there'. The same year he announced, 'I believe that we all came into this world to achieve something. And I think that that's got to be done well. God put us there and gives us a role. One has go to accomplish that work well, however insignificant the job He gives us.'

Whatever the truth, it is clear that Pinochet felt he was living through an apotheosis. This sense of will and of entitlement has allowed him to put his stamp so indelibly upon the country. He did not possess a big enough personality to start a personal cult of the kind that has surrounded other dictators. He lacked the ebullient and overweening egotism of a Fidel Castro, or the flamboyant vanity of a Benito Mussolini, or the warped and evil intellect which, combined with great force of character, marched the whole German people into the abyss of the Second World War.

Only a month before he was killed, Carlos Prats commented on Pinochet's character in a letter written to José Tohá's widow.

> As far as the conduct of Pinochet is concerned, I can tell you that his treason has no parallel in the history of Chile. How can his obliging and affable attitude between March and September 1973 be understood if he himself has recognised his signed undertaking to overthrow Allende that month? The explanation is that in his personality – as in the case of a Duvalier – there admirably comes together a great mental smallness with a great dose of spiritual perversity.

It is a perceptive comment by the man who had once been Pinochet's friend and mentor, and who was to feel the macabre impact of that 'great spiritual perversity' on his own life only a few weeks after this letter was sent.

Assassins

The only credible threat to the Pinochet regime came from abroad, in the form of moderate, non-communist exiles who might be able to form a government-in-exile and gather support from foreign governments.

The three potential leaders of such a movement-in-exile were General Carlos Prats, Bernardo Leighton and Allende's former ambassador to the United States, Orlando Letelier, who had also served as Defence Minister in the very last days of Allende's government. Pinochet decided that all three should be assassinated. The DINA was to carry out the missions.

In Buenos Aires, a city where he had served as Chile's military attaché, Carlos Prats was preparing to write memoirs based on his diaries. From Argentina Prats was kept informed of the situation in Chile by a stream of messages and visits from friends.

In his first diary entry after the coup, written on 27 September, he compared Pinochet's Chile to the most despised dictatorships in America:

'We have', he wrote, 'fallen lower than Trujillo's Dominican Republic, Stroessner's Paraguay or Duvalier's Haiti. We thought we were the most civilised people and today our country is sinking into barbarism.

'The Chilean military and the politicians who pushed them forward, are today living through a moment of triumphalism. Hauliers, doctors, engineers, traders and the ladies with the saucepans, that is to say, our Chilean middle class, believe they have achieved a great victory. We shall see.'

Bernardo Leighton had been one of the founders of the Christian Democrat Party. The Christian Democrat President Eduardo Frei Montalva had appointed him as his minister of the interior. After the coup Leighton was the first to file an application for *amparo*, a version of habeas corpus, in favour of various imprisoned ministers including Carlos Briones, a former interior minister of Allende's. The application was naturally rejected by the judiciary, which was already aligned with the plotters. Nevertheless Leighton had set out his position more by default than anything, as others in his party rushed to welcome Pinochet.

Later in 1973 he and his wife Anita left Chile and settled in Rome at the invitation of the Italian Christian Democrats, at that time the all-powerful party which, with the assistance of the Vatican and the members of the Western alliance, had checked the advance of the Italian communists and controlled Italian politics since the end of the Second World War.

In the Italy of 1974, when rumours of a 'broad anti-fascist front' embracing Christian Democrats and Communists were circulating insistently, Leighton and his former Christian Democrat colleague Rafael Agustín Gumucio, now in the Izquierda Cristiana, or 'Christian Left', issued a call to Christians to join in 'the anti-fascist struggle'. The pronouncement of the friendly, unassuming Christian Democrat who was popularly known as *Hermano Bernardo*, (Brother Bernardo), was praised on Radio Moscow. Leighton was also active in the monthly *Chile-América*, the best of the anti-Pinochet organs published in exile by non-communists.

Orlando Letelier was born in 1932 in the agricultural town of Temuco into a comfortable middle-class family. His father, also Orlando, was the publisher of the local paper and a member of the Radical Party. The family moved to the capital and at the age of fourteen the young Orlando decided to enlist in the army as an officer cadet. In his fourth year he left after a period of illness and decided to take up the law. After his graduation in 1954 he got a job in the copper industry and the following year married Isabel Morel, who was also from a middle-class family.

After a spell working in Caracas he went to work for the Inter-American Development Bank, an institution largely funded by the US government and based in Washington, becoming assistant to Felipe Herrera, the Chilean who was the Bank's president. Slender and handsome, Letelier, and his attractive, dark-haired wife cut a glamorous image. They became friends of Salvador Allende, whom they had first met in 1960. On Allende's victory in 1970 Letelier was a natural choice as the new president's ambassador to the government of Richard Nixon, to whom he presented his credentials in March 1971.

As Nixon and his associates developed their strategy to make life unbearable for the left-wing government in Chile, it fell to Letelier as foreign minister to analyse and suggest ways to Allende of counteracting it. The battle to keep open some lines of credit from the international financial institutions to an increasingly desperate Chile which was becoming ever more desperate for loans was an important item on the agenda of a man who had had Letelier's experience at the Inter-American Development Bank.

Amid the State Department's diplomatic pleasantries and the quiet machinations of Nixon and Kissinger, the embassy premises and the houses of Letelier's staff suffered a series of burglaries in which documents rather than items with a monetary value were stolen. (The same pattern of burglaries was to repeated in 1998 at the Madrid lawyers chambers of Juan Garcés as he worked on the charges against Pinochet.)

As the economic offensive of Allende's enemies, domestic and foreign, escalated, Allende recalled Letelier from Washington in May 1973 to make him foreign minister. Allende then decided to call on Letelier to fill the vacancy left after Pepe Tohá's departure and he was sworn in as defence minister on 28 August 1973.

The murder of General Prats, approved by Pinochet, was the first major foreign assignment for the DINA and Contreras contracted a US citizen to do the job.

Born in Iowa in 1942, Michael Townley had grown up in Chile where his father was general manager of the Ford factory. At eighteen he married a Chilean woman and earned a livelihood selling the dubious IOS mutual funds of the financier Bernie Cornfeld. When the fund scheme failed he was obliged to leave the country. He and his family moved to Miami in 1967 where he mixed freely among the anti-Castro community, whose extreme right-wing views he passionately shared. Townley made an excellent recruit for the DINA. He was Chilean but did not look Latin, he spoke Spanish and English fluently and he had dreams of being a warrior for his country.

Shortly after midnight on 30 September 1974 General Prats and his wife Sofía got in their car outside their flat in the Palermo quarter of Buenos Aires, not far from the Chilean embassy. They had been to a lunch party in the country with friends and then gone on to see a film. Prats alighted to open the door of the garage and returned to drive in. At that moment a bomb exploded, hurling him out of the car and severing his right arm and right leg. His wife burned to death where she sat. Pieces of the vehicle were found on the ninth floor of a nearby block of flats.

Townley, who had worked with Lt. Armando Fernández Larios, another trainee of the US School of the Americas, left that day for Santiago, flying via Montevideo.

With the assassination of Prats, Pinochet had murdered his former commanding officer.

The news of the assassination shocked Chile. In response to popular outrage, the dictatorship put out the story that Prats' murder could only have been committed by anti-Pinochet forces in order to besmirch the Junta. Pinochet immediately announced that Prats' corpse would be buried with official honours. Family friends started preparing the requiem mass. But when the coffin arrived back in Chile the order was given to bring the mass forward and halt the honours. At the church the names of all those present were taken, they were photographed and it was announced that the Argentine government would not be asked to investigate the murder. The case lay uninvestigated until human rights groups took it up again in 1999.

The job of killing the second of Pinochet's major enemies living abroad was also given to Townley. In September 1975 Townley, travelling with a Cuban from the Miami anti-Castro network named Virgilio Paz, set out his plans to an Italian neo-fascist leader, Stefano delle Chiaie. Delle Chiaie had flitted round a number of extreme right-wing organisations such as the Italian Social Movement. He also had links with P2, a masonic lodge which had been linked to a number of crimes and frauds.

On the understanding that the Miami Cubans would claim responsibility for the murder, delle Chiaie, along with Pierluigi Concutelli of the fascist group Ordine Nuovo, who had acted as a paid assassin of Basque separatists for Franco, set the operation up for them. For the Italians, the benefit would be that the joint operation by the Ordine Nuovo and the delle Chiaie's Avanguardia Nazionale would allow them to forge an alliance through this kind of assassination bonding exercise.

Pinochet, as a pupil at
the Academy of War
(*La Nación*)

Pinochet as a young officer, 1940s (*La Nación*)

Before the coup: lorry drivers' strike, outside La Moneda, 1973 (*La Nación*)

After the coup: prisoners in the National Stadium and tanks on the streets.

Pinochet and Allende, September 1973 (*La Nación*)

La Moneda, the presidential palace, under fire from Hawker Hunter jets,
11 September 1973

The Junta, (l to r) Admiral
Merino, Generals Pinochet,
Leigh and Mendoza
(*La Nación*)

Pinochet, wearing the
presidential sash, 1977
(*La Nación*)

General Prats as Commander in Chief of
the Army, decorates Mexican military
attaché, while Pinochet looks on, 1973
(*La Nación*)

Demonstration demanding the release of political prisoners during the Pope's visit to Chile, 1987. The banner reads 'no to the death penalty'.
(*Julio Etchart/Panos Pictures*)

Celebrating in the streets after the results of the referendum of 5 October 1988 (*Julio Etchart/Panos Pictures*)

Voting in
the 1988
plebiscite
(*La Nación*)

Pinochet and his wife, Lucía   (*La Nación*)

Escuela de Caballería, Quillota, December 1990 (*La Nación*)

Pinochet and
President
Patricio Alywin
(*La Nación*)

Pinochet congratulating newly-elected Eduardo Frei Ruiz-Tagle, December 1993 (*La Nación*)

Augusto
Pinochet, 1998
(*La Nación*)

At sundown on 6 October 1975 Leighton and his wife Anita took a taxi back to their lodgings in the Via Gregorio VII, off Rome's Via Aurelia. Amid the noise of traffic the shots of a 9 millimetre Beretta automatic rang out. Leighton fell first; his wife staggered and in her turn fell to a bullet. The gang, directed by Concutelli, melted away into the evening. Townley and his wife set off for London while Virgilio Paz returned to the United States. On 13 October, *Diario Las Américas*, a Spanish-language newspaper in Miami which was close to the anti-Castro community received a communiqué from the Cuban Nationalist Movement claiming credit for the attack.

Although he survived the attack, Leighton was grievously injured. He was never again to exercise political influence. Without him the idea of a centre-left alliance against Pinochet shrivelled.

Although Leighton was not murdered, Pinochet was satisfied. The next month Pinochet made a rare visit to Europe to attend Franco's funeral. The two dictators had earlier exchanged letters of mutual admiration and Franco's allies were happy to have him to swell the meagre ranks of notables at the ceremony. Pinochet was persuaded by Contreras to express his thanks personally to the Italian terrorist in the foyer of the Ritz Hotel in Madrid. For delle Chiaie this was the beginning of an intimate relationship with Pinochet's DINA, which blossomed when he and other Italians of the Avanguardia Nazionale were brought to Santiago as 'consultants' for the DINA and were given Chilean passports.

After a trial in Italy, Colonel Iturriaga, alias Raúl Gutiérrez, head of the DINA foreign operations, was condemned in absentia to 18 years in prison for the assassination attempt. At home, Pinochet promoted him to general.

The job of neutralising Pinochet's third enemy was again given to Michael Townley, who brought together Virgilio Paz and two other extremists from the anti-Cuban lobby, Guillermo Novo and José Dionisio Suárez. The target was Orlando Letelier, now in exile from Chile and working at the Institute for Policy Studies, a Washington-based think-tank.

A bomb was fixed to the underside of Letelier's Chevelle by Townley himself on 17 September 1976 when the vehicle was parked in the driveway of Letelier's house in the suburb of Bethesda. At about 9.15am on 21 September Letelier drove to the centre of the US capital. With him were Michael Moffitt, an economist at the Institute for Policy Studies and his newly-wed wife, Ronni. As the car reached Sheridan Circle the assassination team, following in another vehicle, detonated the bomb by remote control.

In their account of the killing, *Death on Embassy Row*, John Dinges and Saul Landau recount how Michael Moffitt heard a hissing sound, saw a flash of light over his wife's head, then heard a deafening sound. A lawyer passing at the time reported how he had seen a car coming down out of the air.

Letelier's car crashed down onto an adjacent car and came to rest in flames in front of the Rumanian Embassy, leaving behind a trail of destruction. One piece of the car's bodywork was found 82 feet from where the bomb had exploded.

Letelier himself was breathing his last, his head wounded, the lower part of his body blown off. Ronni Moffitt was lying on the lawn, bleeding profusely. An ambulance took Letelier to the nearby George Washington Hospital, but he died before he arrived; a second took Ronni to the same hospital, where she died within an hour of the blast.

In contrast to the operation against Leighton, this assignment was totally successful. The fact that it was executed in the heart of Washington says a great deal about the confidence with which Pinochet was operating in the international arena three years after his seizure of power. The DINA either felt its agents could carry out a spectacular killing in the capital of the United States without being detected, or that the true authors of the crime would be hidden behind a smokescreen of Cuban extremism. Pinochet might well have felt the US government, which had done so much to help overthrow Allende, would take no real action to punish him if the authors of the crime were identified.

Torture

Systematic kidnapping, imprisonment, torture and disappearances continued in Chile long after the first months of the establishment of the new regime.

Testimonies

'For years I wanted to get home urgently after work to see if he had returned.'

'Every time I see a madman or a homeless person in the street I think it might be my husband; or that he might be somewhere in those conditions.'

'They brought my husband in a terrible state to my house to ask me to convince him to talk.'

'Until recently we were waiting for them alive, today we are looking for their bones.'

'I must know what happened to him. I've looked for so long and what happens is that one doesn't know if they might need something, if they are cold, if they want a cigarette. How can I live this way!'

'Why did they take away from me the possibility of being happy?'

'I got married on 8 August and on 5 October I was already a widow. Why did they take away the possibility of being happy with my husband?'

'I was 11 years old, my family disintegrated. At 15 I tried to commit suicide. They took away my childhood. In my house there were never birthdays, Christmas or anything any more.'

'I was 13 and they took me to the barracks to interrogate me and to make me tell them where my father was. I didn't go on studying or anything. All I wanted to do was to die.'

'Our children were different from the rest. We hid the truth from them so they wouldn't suffer. And then they were pointed at because they were the sons of people who had been executed.'

'When my brother disappeared my father was old and he went insane. He died walking in the roads screaming his son's name.'

'I never had the support of my parents. I'm an only child. They applauded the new government and they forced me to sell my house in case my husband returned so that I could never live with him again.'

'I've just met my son again. After the death of his father we were separated for 10 years. I was in jail and he was with my family abroad.'

'My mother was left alone on the farm with my nine younger brothers and sisters, and I had to leave university to work and help her. She has only lived to help her children. I lost my teaching career which was what I most wanted.'

'I looked for my 17-year old son everywhere. I had to do everything on foot because there was no money for the bus. I never heard anything about him.'

'They were arrested because they didn't have an identity card: they were children and they didn't belong to any party because they were almost illiterate. And they shot them.'

'It is frightening to think that one is as much a human being as they are. Where could so much evil come from?'

'After they shot my father, the headmaster called me in and said: you are the daughter of a criminal and therefore you cannot continue to teach in this city.'

'In the school I was told: your father was killed because he was political. We were called the little extremists.'

'I was told he had been freed. Now we have found him in the mass grave with his eyes blindfolded and his hands tied.'

'I was told to bring lunch for my husband. I went and prepared rice with a fried egg. When I returned to the police station he said laughing, 'Lady, you're insane, there's no one under arrest here"

'The first time they searched the house they took us out. My mother was pregnant, They put us against the wall and they simulated an execution.'

Quotations from relatives of victims, in The Rettig Report, the report of the Chilean National Commission on Truth and Reconciliation (The Rettig Commission) 1991

In 1975 one case of torture became particularly notorious. Dr Sheila Cassidy, the British surgeon and the daughter of an Air Vice Marshal in the Royal Air Force, was arrested by the DINA.

She had come to Chile in 1971, wanting a break from an arduous life with at the Leicester Royal Infirmary in England. Cassidy had got work at Valparaiso's San Borja hospital and observed with admiration the government's efforts there to improve the living conditions of poorer Chileans.

Although personally disappointed by the coup, she kept on the right side of the dictatorship for two years. In October 1975 she was called by a Chilean priest, Patricio Cariola, one of the catholic representatives on the Comité Pro Paz, to treat a man with a bullet wound in his leg. She was taken to the house of some nuns from the US. The man turned out to be Nelson Gutiérrez, a leading figure in the MIR. She operated on him as best she could.

Some days later she was detained by DINA agents. She was taken to the infamous Villa Grimaldi on the outskirts of the capital and was interrogated under torture. Her interrogators wanted to know the whereabouts of Gutiérrez, and why she had treated him. Fearing for those close to Gutiérrez, she chose to lie to her torturers.

They checked up on her statements, driving her around the city one afternoon to places she had fabricated. At one moment they took her out of the car and stood her with a guard in the street in the shadow of a doorway. Hearing three young men approaching, she grabbed the grabbed the jacket of one of them and said, 'Help me please, I'm a prisoner of the DINA'. They looked at her with sheer terror and, as the curfew hour approached, hurried on. In her autobiography, *Audacity to Believe*, Cassidy comments, 'My captor struck me hard across the face and I knew that I had been very stupid'.

Her captors took her back to Villa Grimaldi. Cassidy was stripped naked and put on the *parillada* ('barbecue'), an iron bedstead wired up with electric currents.

They took me at once to the room with the bunk and again I was told to undress. The hands that secured me to the metal bed frame were rough and the ropes or straps tied so tightly that my circulation was severely impeded. I asked them to loosen the bonds but they made no response. During the first interrogation I never knew where the electrodes had been placed and the pain was generalized. Now they became more sophisticated for one electrode was placed inside my vagina and the other, a wandering pincer, was used to stimulate me wherever they chose.

From the first moment it was different. The pain was appalling and, determined not to be deceived again, they questioned me with a speed and ferocity that allowed no possibility of fabrication. I don't remember a moment in which I decided to talk but I know that after a while it seemed less likely that my friends would be killed and therefore less urgent to lie. Indeed, I found it quite impossible to lie for the shocks came with such frequency and intensity that I could no longer think. So, they broke me. Little by little I answered their questions. It was a slow and painful business for I told them as little as I could, always hoping that a minimum of people would be involved.

The irony of it all was that they found the truth more difficult to believe than the lies I had told them at first, and I received many gratuitous shocks because they could not believe the nuns and priests were involved. Their disbelief was very hard to bear for there seemed no escape from the white hot sea of pain in which I found myself. Terrifying, too, was the increased callousness of the interrogator. Each time they passed the current a gag was forced into my mouth and I was told, 'Raise your finger when you are ready to talk.' Unable to cry out and with my hands nearly paralysed I could call for relief only through the upward movement of my finger and this they ignored, filling me with a desperation the like of which I have never known.

How long it went on I don't know: perhaps an hour, perhaps longer.

Cassidy was compelled by her torturers to sign a statement on 11 November, before her release saying 'that while I was held in the 4 Alamos detention camp I have not suffered torture or bad treatment. What is more I have had no personal knowledge that other detainees have been tortured, beaten or ill-treated, I declare that I am in a perfect physical and mental state.'

The Labour government withdrew its ambassador from Santiago and imposed a ban on arms sales to Chile, although senior figures in the Conservative Party were unwilling to voice criticism of Pinochet, however terribly the men under his command had treated a British woman surgeon. The diplomatic frigidity was to last until 1980 when the Conservatives were back in power.

When Cassidy's story came out, a senior Conservative MP, the Honourable Nicholas Ridley, who had been a junior minister in the Foreign and Commonwealth Office with responsibility for Latin America, expressed the outrageous view that she could have been exaggerating her experiences. When the Conservatives came into office in 1979, Ridley was among the principal ideological companions of Margaret Thatcher, the new Prime Minister.

Those in the British Conservative Party and elsewhere who played down reports of torture overlook Pinochet's own frank and unalloyed defence of the torture of Marxists and communists. Helmut Frenz, the German Lutheran bishop of Chile who had collaborated with Silva in the Comité Pro Paz testified that when he and the Catholic auxiliary bishop of Santiago Fernando Ariztía met Pinochet in February 1974 he had no qualms about using torture. 'Through other means they wouldn't confess,' he said. Responding to the statement that a priest had been tortured he added, 'He's not a priest, he's a Marxist.'

Operation Condor

Sheila Cassidy's bravery under torture robbed Pinochet and his DINA of one of their most sought-after fugitives. Nelson Gutiérrez, the MIR commander on whose knee Cassidy had operated, eventually escaped by seeking refuge in the Vatican diplomatic mission. The Gutiérrez-Cassidy imbroglio was destined to prompt Pinochet into an international initiative which was to bring him many benefits but also much trouble.

Operation Condor was named after the great bird of prey native to the Andes whose distinctive feature is the collar of white feathers around its neck and its enormous wing span. Among Condor's principal architects were Augusto Pinochet and his deputy Manuel Contreras. Condor was conceived as a co-ordinating committee of the apparatuses of state terror in Chile, Argentina, Uruguay and Paraguay, and to a lesser extent in Bolivia and Brazil.

Its inaugural meeting of leading members of each country's political police took place at the end of November 1975 in Santiago. The quintessence of Cold War thinking was to be found in its initial documents. One, quoted by the Brazilian author Nilson Cezar Mariano in his book *Operación Cóndor: Terrorismo de Estado en el Cono Sur*, commented,

> For some years subversion has been present on our continent, aided by politico-economic concepts which are fundamentally at odds with the history, philosophy, religion and customs of the countries of our hemisphere. The situation described recognises neither frontiers nor countries and infiltration penetrates every level of national life. Subversion has developed a system of command at the intercontinental, continental, regional and sub-regional levels with the aim of co-ordinating actions damaging to society.

Like Chile, Uruguay had fallen under a military dictatorship in 1973. The civilian president Juan María Bordaberry collaborated in a military coup which maintained him as head of state, but closed the congress and gave extraordinary powers to the armed forces. In March 1976 a coup d'état in Buenos Aires also put Argentina into the hands of the military.

The inaugural gathering of the chiefs of each country's security forces was to formalise a more fluid existing relationship. The chairman of the November meeting was an officer of the DINA/CNI, alias Luis Gutiérrez, and his proposal was for the establishment of a head office equipped with a data bank, secure telecommunications capabilities and an operating arm with money, technicians and funds. Condor's organisational model was that of Interpol.

During his visit to Pinochet in June 1976 US Secretary of State Henry Kissinger was made aware of the operation and there is no record of his opposition to it. Indeed personnel involved in the scheme boasted that they had received the gift of a computer from the US adminstration. (The visit of Kissinger and his staff of 80, was a success for Pinochet but not for his wife. Ignored by photographers eager for shots of Nancy Kissinger, Lucía stamped off to her husband and declared, 'Let's go, Augusto. This is the height of rudeness'.)

Kissinger remained a friend of the dictatorship and of Operation Condor. He was someone on whom the regime in Chile could rely. In his book *Cardoen: Industrial o Traficante?* published in 1991 in Argentina and banned in Chile, Juan Jorge Faundes reproduces part of a Chilean cabinet meeting minute, dated 24 October 1979. Signed by Brigadier General Julio Fernández Atienza, the cabinet secretary, it reported a recent meeting between Kissinger and foreign minister Hernán Cubillos. The US official, it said, 'is with the government of Chile, he is a firm anti-communist; he is a notable person who is above everything. He has his doubts about the Pope. He criticised the policy of pushing forward with premature elections in the [Latin American] countries and said verbatim "what do we get out of removing military governments to turn them over to communists. Elections have to be held when stability can be obtained and not when governments are delivered to communists".'

Condor also gave protection to other sorts of criminals apart from murderers. Major José Gavazzo, an Uruguayan officer in charge of OCOA, the Anti-Subversive Command, attempted to get a Montevideo printing firm to print Brazilian 5,000 cruzeiro notes. The counterfeiter was discovered and in January 1995 Gavazzo was sent to jail for 11 months.

In a joint operation on 18 May 1976 Argentine and Uruguayan police seized two of the most important Uruguayan politicians who had sought asylum in Argentina. Senator Zelmar Michelini of the left-wing Frente Amplio was seized at the Hotel Libertad in the centre of the city; his colleague, Héctor Gutiérrez Ruiz, president of the Chamber of Deputies, was seized at the house of a friend from which his captors also stole his personal possessions. Their mutilated corpses were found in an abandoned car four days later.

United in their fight against 'communists,' 'leftists' and 'subversives', the governments supporting Operation Condor successfully controlled the Left in the southern cone, and even elsewhere, throughout the 1970s and 1980s.

For years Operation Condor successfully maintained its secrecy. But in December 1992 a breakthrough came in Asunción, Paraguay. Following the flight of the Paraguayan dictator General Alfredo Stroessner the Paraguayan secret police archives were captured and details of the routine operations of Condor revealed. A document from that archive dated 14 March 1975 and signed by Colonel Benito Guanes, the head of Paraguayan military intelligence, shows the Paraguayan worry about a meeting of left-wingers taking place in the Argentine province of Jujuy and a request for more information. Guanes circulated his document to other Paraguayan authorities and to the military attachés of Argentina, Bolivia, Chile, Uruguay, the US and Venezuela. Similarly, a document dated 4 June 1977 found in the secret police archive in Asunción shows that the Uruguayan Army was seeking Paraguayan help in finding the whereabouts in Paraguay of twenty-two Uruguayan citizens.

Condor's spirit continued well after Pinochet was forced to quit the presidency of Chile, as we shall see later in the case of Eugenio Berríos, but it seems to have finally petered out some time in the mid-1990s. The victims of Condor, including the dead and the maimed, are counted in their tens of thousands.

False judges

'Except in very exceptional circumstances, violations were not investigated by the courts, nor their authors legally punished'.
The Rettig Report, 1991

Within Chile, Pinochet's strategy of terror was greatly assisted by the judiciary's widespread refusal to uphold justice.

With Allende gone and the Congress closed Pinochet knew he had little or nothing to worry about from the third pillar of the state, the judicial power. The Chilean legal system had never taken much of an interest in protecting the rights of its most vulnerable citizens. Pinochet must have realised that the judges were never going to mount a real challenge to him.

At the time of the coup, the Junta made it clear that it would maintain respect for the judiciary, indeed the President of the Supreme Court himself, speaking at the inauguration of the 1974 judicial year, recognised that the judges had been treated well. The judges did complain mildly that Pinochet's first minister of justice was a carabinero, General Hugo Musante, and he was eventually replaced by a civilian lawyer, Miguel Schweitzer.

Nevertheless they comprehensively failed in their wider duties, according to the 1991 Truth and Reconciliation Commission, known as the Rettig Commission. Appeals for *amparo* or habeas corpus were not heard within 24 hours as the law demanded; the courts refused to grant *amparo* to prisoners of the DINA or CNI; there was no enforcement by the courts of the regulation that people may be confined only in their own homes or in public places designated for that purpose. The judges made no effort at all to investigate the many unofficial centres where Pinochet kept his prisoners and whose whereabouts were widely known and often commented upon in the media. They accepted evidence extracted under torture and the validity of that ultimate Kafkaesque abuse of state power, the application of secret laws the content of which were never published. These allowed citizens to be punished for breaking regulations which they could never have known about.

Nor did the judges take any action against those who were continually violating human rights and whose names were often well-known. Nor did the judges exercise their power of supervision over the activities of the courts-martial. When questioned about their passivity, the judges murmured that they too were held in a state of duress and that if they moved out of line they would be sanctioned by loss of seniority, dismisssal, or worse.

The Chilean judiciary never produced any figure who could claim to have even tried to protect human rights during the dictatorship. Its lack of resolve was clear from the first day of the coup. On the morning of 11 September Pinochet sent a bus to collect Enrique Urrutia, the president of the Supreme Court from his home and went on to collect seven others for a secret meeting at the plotters' headquarters.

The next day Urrutia issued a statement. 'The President of the Supreme Court recognises the intention of the new government to respect and enforce the decisions of the judicial power without submitting them to administrative scrutiny beforehand. He announces publicly his most intimate delight in the name of those who administer justice in Chile and expects that the Judicial Power will carry out its duties as it has done hitherto.'

The judges, who had raised all sorts of objections to the actions of the elected government for its supposed breaches of constitution and legality, readily embraced the unconstitutional regime of a group of military plotters.

From then none of the judges accepted one application for *amparo* which involved the armed forces or the DINA. In a time of war, (as Pinochet decreed was the case in Chile) the judicial power could exercise no supervision over the executive.

By December 1973 two decrees codified a state of affairs which had already been in force for weeks. Chile's judges were assigned to three lists. List One was of those who qualified as 'meritorious', those on List Two were deemed 'satisfactory' while those on List Three were 'deficient'. The latter – those who had not shown sufficient hostility to the Allende government – were immediately dismissed without further ado or right of appeal. Others were merely transferred to courts in distant corners of the country.

One particular case was highlighted in Alejandra Matus' book *El Libro Negro de la Justicia Chilena* (The Black Book of Chilean Justice), which was published in 1999 and almost immediately impounded by the Court of Appeal under the Law of the Internal Security of the State.

It tells of Julio Aparicio, an outstanding old man who was the senior justice of the Santiago Court of Appeal and who at the time of the coup was expected to be named to the Supreme Court. After the coup he was appointed state prosecutor in the town of Rancagua, a town a fraction of the size of Santiago 82 kms south of the capital. Because of his age, the humiliation of the demotion and the distance to be covered it was expected that he would not take up the job. In fact he did take it up until his health failed and he resigned, dying shortly afterwards of a heart attack.

In Pinochet's old stamping ground of Pisagua Judge Mario Acuña had better luck. Before the coup Acuña was being investigated for suspected links to a flourishing cocaine trade between Iquique and Bolivia. A visiting magistrate was sent from the capital in 1972 to investigate and he sought the help of the local prosecutor, Julio Cabezas, a forty-five year-old, well-respected local lawyer, who was married with four children. Cabezas favoured the Christian Democrats and was thus an opponent of the Allende government.

The investigation found evidence that Acuña was guilty of fraud and corruption.

Nevertheless, after the coup Acuña was named 'as prosecutor at the local military tribunal. Later he was seen by the cleaner at the local carabinero station giving orders to a group of soldiers who were firing at three men who were attempting escape. At the government offices he was seen giving orders for prisoners' fingernails to be pulled out.

A few days after the coup Cabezas was summoned on the local radio to present himself to the military authorities in Iquique. On 14 September he decided to heed the summons. He left his law students at the courts in the town saying, 'I'm coming straight back. Get on with your cases. I'll look at them when I come back.'

Some of his students insisted on accompanying him to the gates of the Sixth Division where Cabezas stated that an error had been made. The error was his. He was taken off to the camp at Pisagua, which Pinochet had once commanded. Somehow he passed a message to the Council for the Defence of the State in Santiago who had supported the coup and whose representative he was in Iquique. They knew that Cabezas was no leftist, and sent a message to Brigadier General Carlos Forestier, the local army commander, giving Cabezas a clean bill of political health but had no reply.

On 10 October Cabezas' name appeared on a list for a court martial fixed for the next day at Pisagua at 5 am. The Council named one of Cabezas's pupils, Carlos Montoya, to represent him on their behalf at the trial. He flew there that same evening and sought to see his former teacher, now his client, and was told he was not available. Shortly before midnight he was shown documents purporting to be a confession that Cabezas had taken part in Plan Zeta (a supposed leftist plan for violent resistance to the Junta which had no basis in reality. In fact it had been invented by the Junta as a way of justifying its own recourse to violence).

Montoya prepared a rapid defence but the military in charge were too drunk to take account of it. Cabezas was sentenced to death. The camp chaplain told Montoya that Cabezas had already been shot. Years later the army admitted that he and four others had been shot for 'high treason against the fatherland' on 10 October.

Cabezas' skeleton was found in 1990 in a mass grave at Pisagua. In 1988, a case against Acuña, who was proud of his friendship with

General Forestier and General Pinochet, a frequent visitor to Iquique, lingered on in the courts but eventually he was charged with Cabezas' murder. The local Appeal Court found that he was covered by the law of amnesty passed during the dictatorship. He declined into bad health and alcoholism but escaped punishment by the state.

On 3 June 1975 two well-known public figures, Jaime Castillo, a Christian Democrat, and Eugenio Velasco, a Radical, both active on the question of human rights and connected to the church, went to a law conference in Ecuador. The regime took this as a threat, perhaps the beginning of an international confabulation against Pinochet. At 5.30pm on 6 August their offices in Santiago were occupied by men with guns and the two were bundled out without a moment to tell anyone or collect any personal belongings. A LAN Chile flight to Buenos Aires left at 6.10pm. They were aboard in the clothes they stood up in.

The case created a frenzy among Pinochet's enemies in the Santiago middle class, bearing as it did not on some unknown left-winger living in a slum but on two acknowledged leaders of society. An immediate appeal for stay of exile was made to the Appeal Court but the men were already in Buenos Aires.

Within a few days the men's friends and legal colleagues had produced an application for *amparo* larger than anything ever presented to a court. It ran to 226 pages and was presented by twelve lawyers. The well-meaning citizens of the capital flocked to the Supreme Court as the application was presented in such numbers that the carabineros had to strengthen their guards at the door and a loudspeaker was installed for the crowd who could not enter the court to hear the proceedings from outside. It was a clear and massive challenge to the illegalities being practised by Pinochet and his allies on the bench.

The case for the government was presented by Hugo Rosende, an adviser to the interior minister, who declared that the reasons for the expulsions were secret and had to do with national security, adding that there could at any moment be a threat to public order for which the five justices would have to answer. The five solemnly found for the government. One of them died of a heart attack two days later. The day after the judgement Pinochet sent a note of congratulation to Rosende. He later became minister of justice.

Only one application for *amparo* prospered momentarily among the five thousand cases which were refused between the date of the coup and the beginning of 1979. The case created a stir, illustrated the power of the DINA, and showed Pinochet's personal concern about not letting the courts, on the rare occasion when they might embarrass him, get out of his control.

Shortly before midday on 3 November 1976, in the centre of Santiago a man who looked about thirty years old started screaming for help, saying that the DINA had been torturing him. He then threw himself under a bus. The bus driver braked hard and the man escaped death but was laid out, injured, on the pavement by passers-by. A carabinero captain was passing by chance in a jeep and, seeing the crowd and a body on the ground, approached.

As he approached the man started screaming again, 'I'm Carlos Contreras Maluje... Please, help me, the DINA people were torturing me... I escaped... I tried to commit suicide...'

As the captain went to radio for an ambulance and report to his superiors a sky-blue Fiat 125, registration number EG-388, came up and four men in civilian clothes got out. They showed their DINA identity cards and announced they had been looking for him. When Contreras saw what had happened he cried out again to those around him, 'Don't let them take me away! They're DINA! Please, tell my family, Maluje the chemists in Concepción. Carabineros, please help me! Maluje the chemists.'

The four bundled him into their car as he was still screaming, 'I'm Carlos Contreras!' and drove away to an unknown address. Meanwhile bystanders informed Maluje the chemists in Concepción, where spirits rose, and the Vicaría sought *amparo* from the Santiago appeal court, adding the testimony of the eyewitnesses and the captain. The Court made enquiries to the hospital and the forensic medical service but there was no sign of the man.

On 30 January 1977 the Court asked for information from the licensing authority who said the vehicle belonged to the DINA. The next day the Court ordered the minister of the interior to free Maluje immediately. The deputy minister, air force Colonel Enrique Montero, replied that the ministry had no details of the man and that there was no reliable evidence that he had been arrested by the security forces.

At that point Pinochet intervened indirectly, sending a message to the military judge in Santiago on 22 March that he as President of the Republic had convincing evidence that no organisation responsible to him had made the arrest and there was consequently no way of complying with the Court's order.

'The Chief of State has the firm intention of getting to the bottom of the affair which could have been carried out premeditatedly by subversive elements.'

The Supreme Court ordered investigations to continue. They discovered that at the time of the event the Fiat was in the hands of General Enrique Ruiz, the head of air force intelligence. Ruiz replied that he had left the car at 8.30 in the ministry of defence car park and picked it up from there at 2.30am, adding that it was often difficult to observe car number plates accurately and that false number plates could have been used by 'some group which wanted to implicate the intelligence services.'

After questioning General Ruiz, the Supreme Court decided that taking into account the Chief of State's statement there was nothing more to be done and that the case should be closed. The screaming man, Carlos Contreras Maluje, was never heard from again.

Some months later, in January 1977, the DINA was closed down, or more accurately, superseded by the CNI, the National Information Commission. Contreras was replaced by General Odlanier Mena, an officer whose whimsical parents had given him the common first name Reinaldo (the Spanish form of Ronald) spelled backwards. There was nothing whimsical about Mena, however. He continued Contreras' practices but suffered the hardship of not having as much access to Pinochet as his predecessor had enjoyed.

Stranglehold

In the five years after the coup, Pinochet had achieved his aims. He was in complete control of Chile. He had toppled the government, shut the Congress, eliminated the political parties, intimidated a judiciary (which had in any case not needed much intimidation), killed or incapacitated his opponents abroad, overcome his rivals in the army, and escaped sanction or threat from any foreign government.

The arrangements for the emergence of the image of President Pinochet were in the hands of a little-known soldier, Colonel René Escauriaza, secretary-general of the army. Escauriaza had had the benefit of training in the United States. With a friendly style he could tell Pinochet what to wear, when to appear and what to do on public occasions. He arranged ceremonies and parades and could say almost anything to Pinochet, blunting any hurt in his message with a little joke. Pinochet was hard hit when in 1979, at the age of 47, Escauriaza coughed himself to death in an asthma attack.

Escauriaza was aided in his duties by a group of other middle-ranking officers. Also working closely with Pinochet was a media team headed by Federico Willoughby, the Junta's first press officer, and an experienced political team made up of military men and pro-Pinochet civilians. A formal advisory committee to the Junta, the COAJ, was set up at the end of the year. It was made up mostly of army men, despite Leigh's expressed desire to see more air force members in it.

There was also a more mysterious and hidden conclave, the ASEP, the Political Advisory Body, whose members, co-ordinated through General Benavides, did not necessarily know each other. Among their principal members were Miguel Schweitzer and Hugo Rosende, the man who had defended the expulsion of Castillo and Velasco. With its pithy memoranda, prepared for Pinochet in secret, it became, according to the historian Ascanio Cavallo, 'the heart, brains and skin of the government'.

But all was not easy in the corridors of the Diego Portales building. Early in 1977 there was a new outbreak of hostilities between Pinochet and Leigh. Pinochet wanted to establish the post of deputy commander of the army, a position which might be the equivalent of the other three members of the Junta. Leigh refused, saying that the Junta should reach agreement by a majority vote on the question. Pinochet stood his ground. Leigh departed on holiday but was eventually reached by an emissary from the president and, fearful of publicising a damaging split in the armed forces, signed.

In June 1977 Pinochet put forward a decree law conferring legislative powers on the four members of the Junta. But it went on to make it clear that executive power lay in his hands only. He had, after all, taken the title of Supreme Chief of the Nation in June 1974.

In the last days of 1977 the Chilean regime was condemned by the United Nations for its human rights violations. In a swift riposte Pinochet astonished the country as a whole and his three Junta colleagues more than most. He announced that a plebiscite would be called on 4 January 1978 in which every Chilean over 18 would be invited to vote. The electoral registers had long since been ceremoniously reduced to ashes. All that voters had to show was their identity cards which would be clipped and sealed with special tape to indicate that the owner had done his duty. Offices and factories would stop work. The question to which a yes or a no was required was the following:

'In the light of the international aggression unleashed against our fatherland I support President Pinochet in his defence of the dignity of Chile and I reaffirm the legitimacy of the government of the Republic to direct in a sovereign way the institutionalisation of the country.'

The 'yes' box carried the Chilean flag; the 'no' box was a black square. The voting slip was verging on the transparent. Admiral Merino and General Leigh were beside themselves with rage at Pinochet's ploy – about which they had not been consulted or indeed hardly informed until the last moment. The announcement was contained in a Supreme Decree which did not need their signatures. They rightly saw the call for a vote as strengthening still further the personal image of the commander-in-chief of the army as the sole patriotic leader of the nation, leaving the rest of the Junta on the sidelines.

Of the 5,300,000 votes cast, 75 per cent were in favour of Pinochet's plebiscite. This did not relieve the tensions among the four and those between Pinochet and Leigh in particular. Indeed by April preparations were being made within the air force for a coup de force against Pinochet, scheduled for 1 May. The reasoning behind the move was that Leigh was more popular than Pinochet among the armed forces and the country as a whole, and that some commanders of the other armed forces were unhappy with the growing pretensions of commander-in-chief of the army and would side with a pronouncement from the air force.

The prefect of Santiago, carabinero General Germán Campos, had the job of blocking the streets and the bridges across the Mapocho River against any advance by army forces. Eighty men would be sufficient to overcome resistance at the defence ministry. The signal for the coup would be a light plane flying over the centre of Santiago with one wing dipped towards the Moneda palace.

From a conversation during dinner on 30 April at General Contreras' house, General Campos suspected the plot had been blown. He waited in vain the following day for the sign. The air force commanders had lost their nerve and had desisted from their plan for a coup at the last minute.

Leigh's fall was at hand. It was precipitated in July 1978 when he gave an interview to a journalist on the Italian daily *Corriere della Sera*. He called for vast changes to the way Chile was being run. There should be a normalisation of the country within five years; a law to allow political parties to function again; the re-establishment of the electoral register; and electoral law and the preparation of a constitution. He commented that Chile could not continue 'infinitely with liberty being denied'.

The publication of the interview created a political storm in Chile. Pinochet encouraged the cabinet, formally subordinate to a member of the Junta such as Leigh, to write a long letter of complaint to the commander-in-chief of the air force – and announce to the media that they had done so.

On 23 July Leigh's three Junta colleagues met and drafted a message asking him to resign for the sake of the unity of the armed forces. Leigh replied that he had no plans to do so. That was the end: lawyers were called in to draft a decree-law dismissing the recalcitrant airman. He arrived at the Diego Portales building the following day to find it guarded by army personnel in combat dress.

The first of several blazing confrontations came as Pinochet moved to cement his position more formally. To this end he had already formed his own kitchen cabinet of cronies in a bid for uncontested power over his fellow members of the Junta

On 24 July 1978 Leigh was dismissed, to the amazement of most of the senior generals of the air force. His place was taken not by his deputy or his deputy's deputy, but by the tenth most senior officer, Fernando Matthei. In 1998, following Pinochet's arrest, Matthei's daughter Evelyn, herself a senator, who had been elected to the lower house on an extreme-right platform, was to express the family's gratitude by flying to London to appeal for the General's relase.

An international incident

Not only was Pinochet shunned by most foreign governments throughout the 1970s, but Chile itself, and particularly its armed forces, were at the mercy of foreign boycotts.

The British Labour government had halted arms sales. Italy, into whose embassy garden Pinochet's men had dumped a corpse a few days after the coup as a warning to the ambassador that he and his government should not help the Junta's opponents, kept Pinochet at arms length, never appointed an ambassador and was a source of strength for anti-Pinochet Christian Democrats like Leighton. In the United States Senator Edward Kennedy succeeded in halting arms sales to Chile while Pinochet remained in power. The world was a dangerous place for an almost friendless country like Chile, which in 1979 had been so close to war with Argentina that the Vatican was drawn in to find an agreement.

One international incident was to touch a very raw nerve in the Pinochet camp. Just after 2 pm on 21 March 1980, he and his party set off from Pudahuel airport in Santiago on a mission designed to demonstrate to the world that Chile was no longer a pariah state and he was no pariah president.

Pinochet was to make an official visit to the Philippines, accompanied by his wife and daughter, her husband, the foreign minister Hernán Cubillos, and the ministers of finance and defence along with many others. On the way he would stop off for a meeting with Ratu Sir Kamisese Mara, the prime minister of Fiji, one of the more important island countries in the Pacific Ocean, a former British colony and now an independent member of the Commonwealth.

The Republic of the Philippines was not a major world power but, like Chile, had once been part of the empire of Spain. The trip would also underline Chile's aspirations to play a greater role in the Pacific which was beginning a period of rapid economic growth and was an increasingly important market for Chilean exports. The hosts, President Ferdinand Marcos and his wife Imelda, had invited Pinochet to their country three years previously.

The catholic Thomas More University in Manila had declined the government's request to award General Pinochet an honorary doctorate, but another seat of learning was soon found. The envoys of France, Germany and the United States confirmed they would attend the state banquet in Manila, and Filipino and Chilean flags were flying in the capital's streets. Pinochet and Lucía would be lodged at the Malacañang Palace, the official residence of the Marcoses.

General Odlanier Mena had seen to it that there would be good communications between Pinochet's plane, Santiago and the cities on his route. The plane had been in the air for about four hours when the first of two messages arrived. Marcos' ambassador, accredited jointly to Chile and Brazil and who had not been at Pudahuel to see him off, sent a message of good will underlining his president's keenness to welcome him in Manila.

The second came as the aircraft was about to land in Fiji, where it was just after midnight. It was from Charles Le May, the retired rear-admiral who was Chile's envoy to the Philippines. The message was that the Filipino government had cancelled the visit.

Hours before take-off there had been discreet signs that all was not well with the week's programme, despite heroic efforts by teams of diplomats, trade promoters and security men. From the United Nations, General Alfredo 'Macho' Canales, another graduate from the US School of the Americas, had warned that Pinochet might be declared *persona non grata*. Manila had also said that it had been necessary for the speeches at the airport to be cancelled and requested that the General should wear civilian clothes and not uniform. Pinochet had turned down the request flat.

As it turned out, the meeting had been cancelled under tremendous pressure from church groups and unions in the Phillipines, as well as discreet diplomacy on the part of foreign governments. Sweden's Olof Palme had played a particularly important role in lobbying the Phillipine government to call off the meeting.

With little fuel left, the pilot had no alternative but to land in Fiji. There further indignities awaited. There was an ominous delay in getting a gangway to the plane, as workers proved unwilling to move it. The Fijian prime minister, Ratu Sir Kamisese Mara cancelled his meeting with the dictator – in any case it had been arranged at Pinochet's behest. The Fijian government moreover announced that security problems linked to public protests made it impossible for the presidential pair to stay, as planned, at the Suva residence of the governor-general, the local representative of Fiji's head of state, Queen Elizabeth II.

At the airport there were great difficulties in getting the aircraft refuelled, even on payment of a hefty premium. As the party waited on board the captain had to halt the engines, and therefore the air-conditioning, in the interest of saving fuel, thereby gently broiling Pinochet and his fellow travellers in the tropical heat. After the gangway arrived at last, everyone's luggage was minutely checked by Fijian customs officers, who conveniently forgot the English they had learned as former subjects of the British Empire and insisted on reverting to their own language. The only relief for the Chilean presidential party at the airport came when some sandwiches and carbonated drinks came up to the plane by courtesy of the Qantas station manager. To crown it all, on the way to his hotel at 1am, Pinochet's car was pelted with eggs and tomatoes by well-prepared Fijian demonstrators. The only positive factor was that there was little international reporting to transmit the comprehensive debacle to the outside world.

The presidential party were on Fijian soil for less than ten hours that Sunday before they took off once more and limped home via the French island of Tahiti and Chile's own Pacific possession Easter Island.

The following Tuesday, foreign minister Cubillos, whom Pinochet's wife blamed for the affair, was sacked.

IV

Guns and Drugs

'I'll go to heaven. Where would I have gone, do you think? To
hell? No, don't worry, I'll go to heaven.'
Augusto Pinochet, 1989

The first plebiscite

The Fiji débacle of March 1980 touched a very raw nerve within the
Pinochet circle. It showed in the most humiliating way the regime's
lack of political legitimacy abroad. Stung by the widespread
condemnation and fearing international isolation, the dictator's
aides put forward ideas for constructing popular support for the
regime. Pinochet himself appears to have succumbed to the desire
for some form of legitimisation of his rule – as had his predesessor,
military dictator General Carlos Ibáñez, who in the 1930s had sought
popular election to the presidency.

A plebiscite was called. Its date was announced a month before it
was set to take place. All those over eighteen were called upon to
vote on a new constitution. The plebiscite would take place on an
historic day, 11 September 1980, the seventh anniversary of the
1973 coup. There was no restoration of the destroyed electoral
register; votes could be registered in any polling centre in the country
on the production of an identity card. Voting was made compulsory
and, after casting his or her ballot, the voter's thumb was marked
with supposedly indelible ink.

Those who opposed the terms of the new document, elaborated
in secret by Pinochet's appointees, had little chance to organise or
mobilise against it. Voters had to mark a star to assent to or a black
circle to reject the 'New Political Constitution of the Republic of
Chile 1980'. Given the circumstances the result of this farcical
exercise was a foregone conclusion. Of the 6,271,868 votes cast
67.04 per cent were favourable, 30.19 per cent unfavourable and

2.77 per cent were judged to be null. In nine provinces it was reliably estimated that more votes were cast than there could have been voters. When 46 opposition lawyers petitioned the body charged with overseeing the voting, which was made up of Pinochet appointees, it replied that it had no authority to accept complaints.

Chile was left with a document which gave Pinochet a minimum of eight more years in power and sixteen at the outside. From 1990 onward a congress with limited powers would be allowed to function for the first time since the coup. The principal value of the document was that it confirmed to the world that after all his efforts to silence or murder his opponents and rivals, Pinochet, like most dictators, was very anxious to achieve the appearance of democratic legitimacy.

A week after the vote Andrés Zaldívar, President of the Christian Democrat Party, who was at the time on a visit to Jerusalem, received a decree of exile from Pinochet for denouncing the new constitution as illegal. Six months after the plebiscite Pinochet was sworn in as President of Chile for eight years. He installed himself in the newly refurbished Moneda palace, (where in order to protect public morals it was declared that no woman could enter the building wearing trousers).

The new constitution was finally enacted two years later, on the ninth anniversary of the coup. It called for a government candidate to be put up for ratification by popular vote in a plebiscite. In the eventuality that he (it would be a he, as there was little likelihood that a woman would be allowed to stand) were not ratified by the popular will, a new election for a president was to be held.

It did not calm growing public protest. Between May 1983 and July 1986 142 people were killed in demonstrations and protests. After years of dictatorship Chileans were getting tired of Pinochet's discourse and, as was the case in the apartheid regime in South Africa, even leaders of society were weary of being snubbed by foreigners and of being the target of international protest campaigns in Europe. Far from calming public opinion, the plebiscite and the effort to pass off an imposed constitution as legitimate served only as irritants. But there was no sign that Pinochet was willing to surrender any power.

Events came to a head in 1986. In January a brief visit by Senator Edward Kennedy, who had done much in Washington to halt US military supplies to the Junta, was turned into a series of vast street protests against Pinochet. The regime's efforts to counter his popularity by distributing millions of handbills bearing the photograph of Mary Jo Kopechne, who died in his car at Chappaquidick in 1969, had little effect, nor did counter-demonstrations organised by the right. Opposition politicians working clandestinely prepared a document calling for political freedom, *La Demanda de Chile*.

The regime had to move quickly if it was to stifle protest. On 2 July 1986 Carmen Gloria Quintana, 18, and Rodrigo Rojas, 19, were arrested by a military patrol during protests in the Nogales area of Santiago, doused in kerosene and set on fire. Rojas died, but Quintana survived with burns to 60 per cent of her body. The army stated that no troops had been in the area and the government started to refer to it as a United States' sponsored plot, blaming US ambassador Harry Barnes. Unruffled, Barnes attended Rojas' funeral. Seventeen days later the army admitted its crime. Five years later Capt. Pedro Fernández Dittus was sentenced to 300 days in prison for 'failing to summon medical attention' for Rodrigo Rojas.

Worse was to come for Pinochet. On 7 September 1986, four days before Pinochet's thirteenth anniversary in power, the Frente Patriótico Manuel Rodríguez put into effect their Operation Siglo XX (Operation Twentieth Century) which they had been preparing for more than a year.

As Pinochet, his nine year-old grandson Rodrigo and his naval aide-de-camp were returning to Santiago from his country house, the presidential convoy was ambushed by the small guerrilla group. Instant death came to five members of the escort, but the three in Pinochet's car were saved by the armour plating of the Mercedes, the failure of several of the FPMR anti-tank projectiles and the skill of their driver Corporal Oscar Carvajal. Twelve escorts were seriously injured as the Mercedes, crashing past other vehicles which had been hit and were burning, sped back to the house. There Pinochet received treatment for minor cuts on his hand caused by splinters of glass from the Mercedes' armoured windows.

Later that evening the Junta met and a state of siege and an immediate curfew were decreed. Pinochet ordered instant vengeance. The corpses of three known opponents of the dictatorship were found near the Pudahuel airport the following morning riddled bullets. The day after another was similarly shot. In his memoirs Pinochet comments, 'Divine justice was on hand'.

After his escape Pinochet received messages of sympathy from Cardinal Juan Francisco Fresno, the bishop whom the Vatican had appointed as Cardinal Raúl Silva's successor, leaders of other churches, Ronald Reagan, and Margaret Thatcher.

Pinochet went back to overseeing the details of the visit of Pope John Paul II, set to begin on 1 April 1987. But it fell to Fresno and Monsignor Angelo Sodano, the papal nuncio, to deal with Pope John Paul's visit itself. All their diplomatic skills were exercised to try to prevent General Pinochet from transforming the Pope's visit into an act of support for his dictatorship. They nearly succeeded, but the dictator outfoxed them during a visit to the Moneda presidential palace in Santiago, when he manoeuvred the Pope onto a balcony in front of a crowd of hand-picked supporters. Admiral José Toribio Merino, the commander of the navy, even managed to present the pontiff with a model of the Esmeralda, a navy training ship which had been used as a floating torture chamber in the immediate aftermath of the 1973 coup.

During Archbishop Sodano's time as nuncio, relations between the Vatican and the dictatorship and also between the church in Chile and Pinochet improved. This was due in no small part to the fact that in Chile, as elsewhere in Latin America, bishops appointed to vacant sees tended to be more conservative than their predecessors.

The Vatican's support did not, however, give Pinochet the legitimacy he craved. On 30 August 1988, Pinochet had himself proclaimed presidential candidate for the period to 1996 and called upon the people to approve his candidacy. Polling in the second plebiscite took place on 5 October. When the votes were counted Pinochet had achieved only 43 per cent. It would have to go to new elections.

The city of Santiago burst into pandemonium as the news spread. Civilian politicians immediately began to work on elections for the following year. Soon a coalition, the Concertación, was buckled together between the Christian Democrats and those parties of the centre and the left, but excluding the Communists, who had supported Allende. Though still formally banned, the parties had over the years maintained a skeleton structure and were capable of activity. After much bargaining, a cautious Christian Democrat,

Patricio Aylwin, was chosen in preference to the moderate Socialist Ricardo Lagos. Against the Concertación, spanning as it did the centre and the left, no candidate of the right, with or without the blessing of Pinochet, could hope to succeed. Aylwin was elected comfortably, taking over a legitimate presidency from the man who had exercised a dictatorship for fifteen-and-a-half years.

But Pinochet was not to be outdone by a mere popular vote. The Concertación won 71 of the 120 seats in the Chamber of Deputies. In the Senate it gained only 22 of the 47 seats, its majority wiped out, as Pinochet had arranged it should be, by the nine senators he himself had appointed. As long as he held a majority in the Senate the danger of civilian politicians being able to amend the constitution, including the amnesty law which protected the military from being prosecuted for events after the coup, was averted.

A call for arms

'Not a leaf moves in Chile if I don't move it, let that be clear.'
Augusto Pinochet, 13 October 1981

Though Pinochet managed to successfully hold the nation in a state of terror and had eliminated many of his most powerful enemies abroad, the country remained isolated from the respect and community of the nations of the Western Hemisphere. Chile was vulnerable to moral sanction and occasional economic embargoes. The British Labour government had halted arms sales. The Italians never appointed an ambassador.

While Chile continued to suffer boycotts and pressure from international human rights organisations in the 1980s, the munitions needs of the Chilean armed forces still had to be met. In one Carlos Cardoen, Pinochet was to find a large part of the solution to these requirements during the next decade.

The son of a family originating in Flanders, Cardoen was born at Santa Cruz in the Central Valley of Chile in 1940. He turned into a scholarly but ambitious young man, winning a doctorate at a US university, then returned to Chile, where among other things he got a part-time post lecturing to the military. There he caught

Pinochet's attention and with his encouragement Cardoen set up a small factory making light weapons. His bonanza came when war broke out in 1980 between Iraq and Iran. He had the ability to turn out a cheap aerial weapon which could be used with effect against ground troops by armies without advanced technology. The sales brochure, produced in Spanish, English, French and Arabic said it all:

> The Cardoen cluster bombs are the most effective modern armament systems for use against targets dispersed over wide areas.
>
> Low or high altitude attacks at high speed can produce devastating effect without requiring pin-point accuracy.
>
> After being dropped, the bombs are opened in midair by an electronically programmed fuze and a number of sophisticated bomblets are released (50 in the CB-130 lb and 240 in the CB-500 lb).
>
> The surface area covered by the bomblets has an elliptical shape of some 15,000 to 50,000 square metres, depending on the size and the operational use of the bombs.

The weapons were perfect for use by Saddam Hussein against the Shiites, and he bought them by the thousand. The contract was the making of Cardoen. There was, however, one tragic moment. On the morning of 25 January 1986 there was an explosion on the assembly line at the bomb factory in Iquique. Nearly 1,500 bomblets about to be assembled into the main bombs exploded, killing 29 men. In an effort to reassure the traumatised city Cardoen declared, 'The next bomb to be assembled will be assembled by me.'

Cardoen went on to work with a Spanish company on what was labelled 'the poor man's atomic bomb', a device known as Fuel Air Explosive which, it was claimed, was five times more powerful than TNT, killing humans by gobbling up the oxygen around the point of its detonation.

But his activities were not confined to munitions or to the Middle East. He also manufactured a range of small armoured vehicles, one called Escarabajo, 'Scarab', and another, Alacrán, 'Scorpion'. Armoured vehicles were also produced under licence from the Swiss company MOWAG.

He sold his cluster bombs to President Mengistu Haile Mariam of Ethiopia until the deal was halted by Pinochet's civilian successors. A deal was also signed with ARMSCOR, the arms manufacturer created by the apartheid governments of South Africa.

There was a public-sector effort as well. The army's own weapons manufacturing unit was called FAMAE. In association with Ferrimar, a privately owned engineering company, it made a pitch to the Iranians for the supply of its own aerial weapon, WB-500-F Avispa, or 'Wasp'. After negotiations carried on directly with Teheran through the London office of the National Iranian Oil Company opposite Westminster Abbey, a deal was clinched. But the test staged in Iran turned out disastrously. The weapon gravely damaged the Iranian Phantom F-4 which launched it over the skies near Teheran. The furious Iranians demanded compensation.

FAMAE's agreement in 1988 with British Ordnance for the development of an unsophisticated but serviceable rocket called Rayo – 'Lightning Flash' – went better. Pinochet was particularly proud of Rayo, not least because it brought him closer to the British whom he so admired. It had a range of up to 35 kilometres and was tested in Wales and northern Chile. The president had successfully ensured that his country was not to be left to the mercy of foreign arms salesmen.

Chile's developing arms capability allowed it to breach the UN embargo on sales of arms to the contending sides in Yugoslavia and sign a contract for the delivery of arms to Croatia at the end of November 1991, three months before Chile recognised that country as independent from Yugoslavia. (The consignment's documents first said it was bound for Nigeria, then they were changed to show that the final destination was to be Sri Lanka. The Boeing 707 carrying the rifles and ammunition, missiles and their launchers and mortars with their mortar bombs eventually landed in Budapest where the Hungarian authorities promptly impounded them.)

The following month Deputy Jorge Schaulsohn of the left-of-centre Party for Democracy, PPD, called for a parliamentary investigation of the affair, hinting that Augusto Pinochet Junior who headed the firm PSP which was in the arms business, could have been involved in the transaction. Colonel Gerardo Huber, the army officer responsible for the Croatia shipment who had previously been working at the army's chemical warfare plant at

Talagante, was apparently found dead some weeks later. It was announced he had committed suicide but the fact that the army seized his body from the forensic scientists gave rise to rumours that he was still alive.

Into this burgeoning arms business an even more dubious trade was being spliced. The connection of the Pinochet regime to narcotics had long been known about by those who follow Chile closely. In their 1980 book about the murder of Letelier *Assassination on Embasssy Row*, Dinges and Landau, whose sources in the FBI were excellent, reported that Manuel Contreras had set up protection for drug dealers with the profits going to the DINA and to the Cuban anti-Castro lobby.

There was little more published on this topic until an article in the 21 January 1993 number of *Análisis*, a Santiago magazine which was closed down shortly afterwards. With help from Chilean police sources it recounted the activities of a Santiago company, Chile Motores. Its trade included the import of second-hand diesel engines for installation in the capital's buses. A close member of Pinochet's family and a businessman of Middle Eastern ancestry, Yamal Edgardo Bathich Villaroel, were shareholders. This partnership, said the article, broke up in 1989 and Bathich went abroad.

The following year a Colombian with strong connections to the drug business, Jesus Ochoa Galvis, came to settle in Chile and took an interest in the motor company, now renamed Focus Chile Motors. The company still retained its link with Bathich, a close friend of Monzer al-Kassar, a Syrian arms dealer convicted in London for drug offences and subsequently denied entry to Britain, and with lawyers linked to leaders of the UDI, the extreme right-wing pro-Pinochet party.

On 3 June 1992 Bathich was arrested by Spanish police at Madrid airport with al-Kassar, but Bathich was released shortly afterwards. On 7 December 1992 the Chilean tax authorities, acting on a tip-off, raided the premises of Focus Chile Motors but were denied access to its accounts.

Later that day they returned with carabineros and placed seals on boxes and drawers containing documents and a carabinero guard was left at the entrance. When they returned two days later, after a public holiday, they found that the seals had been broken and a quantity of burnt documents smoking outside. A search by the squad dealing with drugs and economic offences on 10 December discovered an arsenal of revolvers, sawn-off shotguns, an Uzi machine pistol and other pistols, ammunition and body armour. It was also discovered that the company had access to a helicopter pad and two helicopters; Bathich, it turned out, was an enthusiastic helicopter pilot. Bathich left Chile on 9 December and Ochoa left two days later.

The article, though interesting, did not substantiate any charges of drug-dealing, though it hinted very strongly that it had been the business in hand. New material was later discovered which gives a convincing picture of a long-standing relationship between the dictatorship and the narcotics world-a connection to which Dinges and Landau had pointed in 1980. In their book the authors referred to Pinochet's knowledge of the narcotics situation and the relationship between the Chilean dictatorship and anti-Castro militants and their collaboration on murder missions. 'Pinochet turned over to the United States drug enforcement administration a planeload of cocaine dealers rounded up after the coup... Then Pinochet's right-hand man, Contreras, could set up his own men with DINA protection in the same factories and shipping points. The anti-Castro Cubans had a piece of the action. The enormous profits went to supplement DINA's clandestine budget.'

Pinochet often claimed that he controlled the DINA – and indeed, as the famous quotation at the head of this chapter testifies, all that happened in Chile. In February 1998 Manuel Contreras made his statement to the Supreme Court implicating Pinochet in every action of the DINA. The statement, of great use in the subsequent prosecution of Pinochet, made clear, if any further clarification has been needed, of the relationship between the dictator and his secret police. 'As Delegate of the President,' Contreras declared, 'I constantly informed the President of the Republic of any activity or event that arose, at the moment of its occurrence as well as daily. At the same time, you can recognise my absolute subordination to and dependence on the President of the Republic.

'I always carried out satisfactorily the orders that the President of the Republic gave me. Only he, as the Superior Authority of the DINA, could arrange and order the missions that were executed, and always, in my capacity as Delegate of the President and Executive Director of the DINA, I carried out strictly that which I was ordered to do. The President had the standing order that he be informed daily of any important news, and at the same time, as standard doctrine, that he be informed constantly of the implementation of orders given. I worked in direct subordination to the President of the Republic and Commander in Chief of the Army, without any intermediary.'

In the light of his own and of Contreras' statements it would be fanciful to imagine that the dictator lived in ignorance of the narcotics situation. This was also a time when US administrations were intensifying their 'war on drugs', making it the main item on their agenda for relations with Latin America.

Frankell Baramdyka – outstanding US marine, expert drug smuggler

New information on narcotics came in the form of a man extradited by Chile to the United States at the beginning of May 1993. Frankell Baramdyka is a man of faces and disguises. He travelled to Chile on a US passport which gave his date of birth as 25 November 1953 and his place of birth as Greece. He has also used the alias of 'Trinidad Moreno', speaks fluent Spanish and has good knowledge of Colombia and the Caribbean. He once claimed he was 'a poor Colombian boy'.

Authenticated documents from the US Marine Corps show Frankell Baramdyka had an excellent military record. On 15 December 1976, for instance, his commanding officer at the Marine Barracks in San Diego awarded Corporal Baramdyka a testimonial which said 'your display of industry, maturity and leadership far exceeded that expected of a Marine of your rank' and added, 'Through your military bearing, courtesy, tact and sound judgement you have been an asset to the United States Marine Corps'.

Baramdyka's difficulties came when he turned those talents to the drug business. His drug connection started in Los Angeles in the 1980s. He claimed he had moved drugs and money around Central America and the Caribbean on the orders of various officers of the US forces for the benefit of the Contra terrorists who were seeking the overthrow of the Sandinista government of Nicaragua.

Donald Gene Henthorn and William Horner Lawrence, both pilots, were indicted with him by the grand jury for their part in transporting several tons of drugs on US aircraft.

On 12 May 1985 Baramdyka's house in Los Angeles was raided by the police on a tip-off from one Ferris Ashley, who had been arrested with two kilograms of cocaine and said he had been working in Baramdyka's drug-selling ring. The police found no drugs in Baramdyka's house but did find US$425,000 whose source he could not justify. (In evidence Baramdyka claimed the sum found was actually US$600,000.)

On 23 May, Alicia del Carmen, Baramdyka's Chilean wife, arrived by air in Chile with her two children with a Chilean passport issued in her maiden name a few days earlier by the Chilean consulate-general in Los Angeles. A month later she joined the list of shareholders of a fishing venture which had for some months been registered in Santiago under the name Redes del Pacífico, 'Pacific Nets'. Other shareholders included one Federico Humberto Silva. Silva was supposedly an officer of the consulate-general and bore a Chilean diplomatic passport. His name did not however figure on the Chilean foreign ministry's list of diplomatic staff or locally employed staff though his father, Fernando Silva, was at the time director of the ministry's frontier department. Various witnesses had seen Federico Humberto Silva at work in the offices of the consulate general.

Alicia del Carmen was followed to Santiago by her husband Frankell on 22 June 1985. He had managed to give the US the slip. For a time Baramdyka, alias Trinidad Moreno, worked in the Chilean capital as general manager of Redes del Pacífico, building himself a large house in Santiago and driving a Cherokee 4x4. The company's bank account showed an annual turnover of the equivalent of US$4 million, some 90 per cent of the deposits being made in cash.

On 19 March 1987, Federal District Court in San Diego, California, asked the Pinochet dictatorship to arrest and extradite Baramdyka on evidence that Redes del Pacífico was engaged in the trafficking of cocaine. He was arrested at the company's offices on 14 May and while he was in custody was several times interrogated by officials of the US Drug Enforcement Agency and the US Customs. The US authorities alleged in the documents supporting their application for Baramdyka's extradition from Chile that in

1984 and 1985 he had brought 1.5 tons of cocaine into their country through the Mexican territory of Baja California.

On 22 December 1987 the Supreme Court of Chile decided he could be extradited. But the Chilean state would not let him go. Before he could be flown back to the US he had to face charges, real or imaginary, in the Chilean courts relating to cheque frauds and on 26 July 1989 he was condemned to five years and one day in prison on those charges. Strangely, while he was in prison in Santiago he was seen to be in possession of large quantities of cash and appears to have had enough money at hand to have been able to pay back the sums involved in the dud cheques. He was released on 26 January 1993 and at the beginning of May the civilian government which succeeded Pinochet finally extradited him to California.

While imprisoned in Santiago Baramdyka had been in contact with various print and media reporters to whom he told his story. He certainly showed great familiarity with the operations of the Colombian drug world, the Contras in Central America and the drug dealing in which they and their allies, particularly the military of Honduras, were engaged. He also named various US military officers who he said were involved in what became known as the Drugs for Guns operation. Baramdyka admitted that in 1984 and 1985 he had flown into Baja California from Colombia with three consignments of cocaine totalling 1,650 kilograms which were later sent on to California. He worked with Michael Pittman, a former pilot for a large US airline. In his sworn deposition to the US court in San Diego, which was included in the US application for Baramdyka's extradition, Pittman said of events of 29 October 1984 in a cafeteria and bowling alley in Los Angeles, 'I met Frankell Ivan Baramdyka, who then hired me to fly a load of cocaine from Colombia to Mexico for $100,000.'

Through his Chilean wife and through contacts with the Chilean consulate-general Baramdyka said he became aware of the opportunities for the narcotics trade in Chile. He claimed his Colombian contacts had been supplied with raw materials for the development of cocaine by the Chilean Army's chemical works, the Complejo Químico Industrial at Talagante, and added that he had given US$2 million to a member of the staff of the Chilean consulate-general in Los Angeles on behalf of Colombians in payment for the goods.

After settling in Santiago in June 1985 he continued his narcotics trading down new avenues. In October of that year he told reporters that he had been approached by a major and a captain in the Chilean army (whom he named) who said they knew exactly what business he was in and asked him to find a buyer for 75 kilograms of cocaine. This he did, working with a Cuban associate in an insurance company in Miami. The price was US$43,000 per kilo. 'I think this was a test', he commented.

In December 1985, Baramdyka claimed he met with Edgardo Bathich and others in Santiago. Bathich claimed to have good contacts at the top levels of government and with the intelligence services. He also claimed to be importing cocaine from Brazil hidden in second-hand car engines and via lorries and helicopters from Bolivia. A certain amount was being re-exported to the US with the help of airline staff but now the time had come to move much larger quantities.

A few days later Baramdyka told journalists that he had been called to the armed forces headquarters in the Alameda to an interview with 'Colonel Gutiérrez', the pseudonym always used by the heads of the DINA/CNI foreign operations. Baramdyka gathered that 'Gutiérrez' was the director of narcotics operations. He answered directly to General Humberto Gordon, the then-chief of the CNI, whose post was later taken over by General Hugo Salas Wenzel. He confirmed to Baramdyka what Bathich had reported. A related problem, said 'Colonel Gutiérrez', was that things were going wrong in Stockholm.

From the beginning of the Pinochet era the Swedish capital had been the principal European base for the terrorist and drug-related activities of the DINA/CNI. Many Chilean exiles had been welcomed to Sweden since the first days after the coup, when Ambassador Harald Edelstam had heroically dashed around Santiago extending asylum to those who resisted Pinochet's putsch. The regime felt there were many Chilean exiles in Sweden who needed to be spied upon, but Pinochet had a personal reason to choose Stockholm as a base for his secret police operations. He was particularly bitter towards Prime Minister Olof Palme and his Social Democratic Party for their part in the Fiji/Philipines debacle of 1980. But, said 'Colonel Gutiérrez', CNI operations of all types in Europe had to be found a better home.

Two months later Palme was dead, shot on the evening of 28 February 1986 as he and his wife Lisbet came out of a cinema in the centre of the capital. The prime suspects for the killing were declared to be the Kurdish community. Nevertheless the possible link between the Pinochet regime and the murder of the Swedish prime minister was also investigated by the Swedish authorities, as I wrote in *The Observer* in June 1986. One senior member of the Swedish government said that the investigators had information that Townley had been given the job of arranging Palme's death as long ago as 1975, and the Swedes had sought help from the US Department of Justice and the FBI to find the murderer. Following the report in *The Observer* the Chilean foreign ministry issued a statement denying Chile had any part in the murder. The CNI connection to the Chilean embassy in Stockholm, as set out by an experienced drug dealer, cannot but strengthen the long-standing Swedish suspicions about Chilean involvement in the killing of Palme.

By September 1985 Baramdyka found himself on CNI business in Madrid, where he set about organising a new cocaine sales network to substitute for the Swedish centre. One of his contacts was a Chilean officer who had been previously stationed in Stockholm.

In March, June and October 1986 and in March and June 1987, Baramdyka said, he arranged numerous flights from Chile in which shipments of cocaine with a total weight of 12 tons were packed in with consignments of cluster bombs to Iran and Iraq. The packages were made up at the Chilean army's arms plant, FAMAE, in Santiago, sent on army vehicles to the international airport at Pudahuel and dispatched abroad. The drugs were then off-loaded for sale in Europe at intermediate stops, often the airport of Port-au-Prince, the capital of Haïti, or in the Canary Islands. One of the aircraft used for the shipments, which had been chartered by a British registered company Quinn Freight, was the one which took Robert McFarlane and Colonel Oliver North to Iran on 25 May 1986 for talks on the Iran-Contra deal. In his memoirs North refers to the aircraft as 'our disguised Israeli 707'.

In his statements in prison, Baramdyka threw new light on the mysterious death of Jonathan Moyle, the 28 year-old British helicopter pilot whose corpse was found by a chambermaid hanging in a cupboard in room 1406 of the Carrera Hotel in Santiago on the morning of 31 March 1990.

It was a bizarre scene. The cupboard was not tall enough to allow him to hang himself, even had he wanted to. He was semi-naked and was wearing what was described as 'a bulky nappy-like garment'. An empty syringe was on the bedside table.

No satisfactory explanation emerged about the death of a young man who had served in the Royal Air Force with notable success. While holding a student scholarship from the RAF, Moyle had won a first-class honours degree in international relations and strategic studies at the University of Wales at Aberystwyth. During his time at university, according to his biography *The Valkyrie Operation* published in London in 1998, he had worked for Special Branch, the British political police, reporting on his fellow students. Aberystwyth was seen to be a stronghold of Welsh nationalism and Special Branch took action following Moyle's tip-offs.

He also informed on those students who were using cannabis. His biographer, Wensley Clarkson, writes, 'Many students strongly objected to Jonathan taking such a high moral tone about so-called soft drugs. But the young RAF student saw it all in very black and white terms. He had absolutely no interest in taking drugs and couldn't understand why anyone would even want to experiment with them. They were illegal and that meant he had a duty to expose anyone who was involved with them.'

While still in his early twenties Moyle found himself in the planning department of the Ministry of Defence. Although he had qualified as a pilot, he was refused flying duties and he later left the RAF to work as at a newsletter called *Defence Helicopter Weekly* as a journalist. He had been in Santiago at the time of his death writing for this publication about FIDAE 90, the regular air and space show that is held in the Chilean capital every two years. During the show he was noticed in company with senior figures in the Chilean arms trade who were later to be identified as organisers of drug trafficking. His exchanges with them appeared to be stormy.

Rumours were passed around at a reception in the British embassy in Santiago and reproduced in the British press, that Moyle had killed himself in the course of dangerous sexual practices which involved getting as close to death as possible. The allegations were angrily denied by his father Tony. The family pointed out that Moyle was shortly to be married to his German girlfriend Annette Kissenbeck, a paediatrician, with whom he had been in touch by telephone only hours before his death and whom he had accompanied to buy her wedding dress less than a month before.

In the House of Commons the Conservative Prime Minister Margaret Thatcher was asked by left-wing Labour MP Ken Livingstone whether she would respond to a statement from a Chilean investigating judge that British officials had been unwilling to co-operate in a proper investigation of the death. The Prime Minister refused. In the Commons a junior minister at the Foreign and Commonwealth Office, Timothy Sainsbury, went on to attack as 'irresponsible' Malcolm Coad, the Santiago correspondent of *The Guardian* newspaper, who had published details of attempts by British officials in Santiago to blacken Moyle's name. The impression was that both the British Government and the newly-installed civilian government in Santiago were keen to have Moyle's death forgotten as quickly as possible.

According to Baramdyka, Moyle had been killed because in the course of his investigations of the Chilean arms industry for Defence Helicopter Weekly he had found evidence of Chilean drug trafficking and its link with arms exports of the sort Baramdyka was familiar with. In prison awaiting extradition the former US Marine speculated about whether he would suffer a similar fate. 'Jonathan Moyle', he said, 'found out that at a refuelling stop of an aircraft flying from Chile with arms they unloaded eight or ten packages loaded with cocaine. And he followed up his investigations without telling anyone, or consulting anyone, and that cost him his life.'

There is no doubt that Moyle had included drugs, an early preoccupation of his, in the list of interests in Santiago. In the week after the air show he had been due to visit Bolivia to observe the operations of the US Drugs Enforcement Agency in that country.

Baramdyka's evidence raises questions about how much the British, US and other governments knew about the drug trafficking being run from Chile. It would surely have been a serious oversight on the part of their intelligence services if they knew nothing. If they did know of the trafficking, why did they not halt it with alacrity, as they would have done if such practices had been detected in countries other than Chile?

Further evidence of Chilean official involvement in drugs, unconnected with Baramdyka's statements, comes from the strange case of the disappearance of Eugenio Berríos, the man whom secret police chief Manuel Contreras had called 'our mad scientist'.

Using raw materials imported from England, Berríos, a right-wing extremist who had joined the DINA in 1974 and whose code name was Hermes, had been manufacturing the nerve gas sarin for the Chilean army at its chemical warfare plant at Talagante. In *The Observer* in 1989 I reported how the Chilean bought equipment from A. Gallenkamp, a company based in Loughborough, in the English Midlands. Gallenkamp's parent company Fisons claimed it could find no record of the sale. He also bought microwave equipment in Miami.

The Chileans' possession of sarin, produced in what was called Operation Andrea, was a matter of international concern in the 1980s; the Green Party in Germany was particularly assiduous in pressing the government in Bonn to investigate the connection. In their book about the murder of Letelier, *Labyrinth*, Taylor Branch and Assistant US Attorney Eugene Propper recount how the first sarin trials began in late 1975 and the first useable product was produced the following year. The tactical importance of the weapons for the Chilean army, say the authors, was to guard the relatively short frontier with Peru and also to guard the Andean passes further south. through which Argentine troops could march.

Berríos, according to Baramdyka, was later involved in experiments to produce an odourless form of cocaine which would evade detection by sniffer dogs and electronic devices. An erratic character, he had quit Chile at the end of 1991 and entered Uruguay, apparently illegally, with the help of the Chilean and Uruguayan intelligence services. He left his young wife Gladys behind in Santiago.

Berríos, himself a heavy cocaine user, seemed to lead a normal life in Uruguay but something went wrong on 14 November 1992. He rushed into the Parque del Plata police station in Montevideo in a disturbed state and appealed for help after shouting, 'Pinochet has given orders to kill me!' He was taken from police custody at the station by Captain Eduardo Radaelli, an officer in the Uruguay's military counter-intelligence. He was last seen alive in December 1992 in the Uruguayan capital.

Details of the incident at the station and the fact that it had not been officially recorded by the police at the time were published in the Uruguayan press in June 1993. The matter was of such importance that it forced Uruguayan President Luis Lacalle to rush back to Montevideo in the middle of an official visit to Britain. On his return the Uruguayan president sacked his friend General Oscar Aguerrondo from the post of head of military intelligence.

Berrios' corpse was found half buried on El Pinar beach near Montevideo on 13 April 1995. Forensic scientists judged that he had been shot twice in the head around March 1993.

In October 1998, Juan Fagúndez, the lawyer representing the Berríos family, claimed that the murder of Berríos was linked to the private visit of Pinochet to Uruguay in March 1993. Berríos, he said, was considered by the Pinochet regime as 'out of control and dangerous'. He declared 'among the soldiers who accompanied Pinochet are the killers of Berríos.' The case was adjourned indefinitely by Judge Alvaro González in Uruguay on 27 November 1998, although he added it could be re-opened if new evidence were produced. The file would, he said, remain secret.

Banking on torture

From the first day of the coup Pinochet forged an excellent relationship with financiers who were delighted by Allende's demise. Bankers were the first organised group to give an international welcome to the seizure of power of General Pinochet. They were also among the first to benefit from Pinochet's regime.

After the coup there were fears – or hopes, depending upon which side one stood – that the Inter-American Development Bank, the IDB, would cancel the meeting it was scheduled to hold in Santiago in April 1974. These hopes were misplaced. The IDB was, and remains, a large international financial institution based in Washington and owned by its member governments. Its raison d'etre is to lend money to countries of Latin America whose governments respect the orthodoxies of international finance. The United States is its most important shareholder, and there are few occasions when it acts contrary to its political strategies.

The institution has been quick to suspend the funds of those Latin American governments who have asserted too great independence from the will of Washington. IDB funds were cut off from the Peruvian government of General Juan Velasco after he nationalised the US-owned International Petroleum Company in the 1960s. Nicaragua, a habitual beneficiary of IDB funds under the Somoza dictatorship, was denied more monies when the Sandinista revolution created a new government in Nicaragua in 1979. Indeed Allende had been starved of international funds at the behest of President Nixon.

After the coup, many senior bankers from the western hemisphere and Europe were happy to make the acquaintance of the Pinochet regime. The regime itself also did its best to seize the initiative on economic matters. An economics group within the new regime was headed by Roberto Kelly and Hernán Cubillos, two former naval officers who were among the circle of admirers of the free-market doctrines of the University of Chicago whose leading light was Milton Friedman.

The economy that Pinochet had seized was not in good shape. The first two years of Allende's rule were very satisfactory, economically speaking, with workers' wage levels easily outstripping inflation. By 1973 however the US campaign to starve Allende of foreign loans was succeeding, despite the willingness of European countries and banks to supply some of the lost credit. The deliberate economic sabotage carried out in 1973 left the economy in ruins. By the time Pinochet seized power, inflation was running at an annual rate which was difficult to estimate with accuracy but was somewhere between 500 and 650 per cent.

The final nail in the coffin of the Chilean economy was struck when the world price of copper fell. This pushed the balance of payment deficit on the current account from US$114 million in 1970 up to nearly $640 million in 1972. In terms of its economy Chile was bleeding to death.

The first economy minister named by Pinochet was Fernando Léniz, president of the *El Mercurio* newspaper, which had for the previous three years been carrying on an energetic campaign against the elected government, sustained by a subsidy of $1.5 million from the government of the United States. The principal shareholders of *El Mercurio* were the Edwards family, the descendants of early 19th century immigrants from Britain who had founded a banking empire, the Banco de A. Edwards, and further increased their wealth as the salesmen of a popular brand of American carbonated drinks.

In the workplace

The Miners Federation gave us a copy of Decree Law 198. In short, it bans the election of officers. It provides for the automatic filling of vacant posts by the co-option of senior workers. Each factory sends a list of its 15 oldest workers, the Junta then chooses five to represent the factory.

Further elections are prevented by the automatic extension of terms of office; meetings during working hours are forbidden; meeting outside working hours are subject to military control (a written request to hold a meeting and a copy of the agenda has to be submitted to the local police, 48 hours in advance. Either a policeman or military man always attends the meeting); the right to draw up union rules is banned; the right to strike is banned; the right for collective bargaining is banned; the arbitration and negotiating committees have been abolished; the *fuero sindical* guaranteeing union leaders protection from arbitrary wrongful dismissal suspended (claims of wrongful dismissal are examined by a committee of military officers); the right to collect union dues is banned.

Even if a union exists, virtually all genuine activity is obstructed.

Though some unions, such as the Miners' Federation, continue to exist, without funds their activities are very limited. Contact with their membership is extremely difficult, not only because they have to meet in semi-clandestinity, but because they do not have the finance to travel to the mining areas regularly.

Trade union and human rights in Chile and Bolivia, Report of the National Union Mineworkers delegation, 1977.

Léniz and his associates pushed through an immediate programme to favour richer Chileans by cutting taxes and public spending, a strategy which undid much of the progress which the Allende government had achieved in making Chile into a fairer society with opportunity for all. Léniz abolished taxes on wealth and capital gains tax, giving the wealthy a chance further to enrich themselves and widening the already enormous gulf between rich and poor in Chile. At the same time the privatisation of much of the economy provided golden opportunities for those who were able to take part in that process, notably, as we shall see, the Pinochet family itself.

Allende's price controls, which had kept basic items within the reach of poorer people, were abolished by the dictatorship at a stroke. Trade union activity was hampered where it was not totally outlawed, and stripped increasingly vulnerable workers of protection.

Land reforms pursued by both Frei and Allende were reversed and land returned to its former owners, causing rural workers to suffer. The free daily ration of milk which Allende had set up for children was abolished, and health services and the state school system deteriorated. Unemployment, which in the Allende years had been around 4 per cent of the workforce, touched 14.5 per cent by 1975.

In the same year the gross national product dropped by 12.9 per cent and the average Chilean grew 20 per cent poorer, with those at the bottom of the social pyramid losing out most. Yet still inflation soared; the official index of consumer prices rose by 340 per cent in 1975. Aid agencies reported that children going to school without food were fainting in the middle of classes.

In the mid-1970s Pinochet's policies produced a striking image for the times, the soup kitchen. These informal food banks filled a great need for poor Chileans. It was common in the poor neighbourhoods that surroundied many cities to see long queues of people lining up for dollops of food among their leaking wooden shacks and unmade roads.

In 1975 Milton Friedman visited Chile in the company of another right-wing economist, Arnold Harberger. Both proclaimed themselves satisfied with the state of the Chilean economy. Meanwhile, the bankers who had so cannily smelt good times coming in September 1973 made hay. In her study for the Economist Intelligence Unit in 1987, Stephany Griffith-Jones, the eminent Chilean economist, pointed to how the bankers were making enormous profits on their loans. In the second half of 1975 they paid depositors 19 per cent a year in real terms while they charged borrowers on average 115 per cent for loans, a margin of 96 per cent. In 1976 the margin shrank from this astronomic rate to the merely excessive rate of 51 per cent.

Those who had money to put on the stock exchange or into land – the tiniest minority of the population – saw their wealth multiply wildly. In real terms, that is, discounting inflation, the share price index went up ninefold from 113 in 1975 to 1,012 in 1980. The index of the price of urban land went from 240 in 1976 to 872 in 1981. Foreign bankers rushed to lend to Chile.

In 1981 the boom started to turn to bust. The price of copper fell by 40 per cent between 1979 and 1982. Chile's earnings for its exports were swiftly overtaken by the size of the bill for its imports. In 1981 two banks and six other institutions had to seek the support of Pinochet's government. In August 1982 the Chilean currency, now renamed the *peso*, had to be devalued from 39 cents to the US dollar to 46 cents to the dollar. Those who had borrowed in foreign currency could often no longer service their debts and those foreign investors who had rushed to put money into Pinochet's Chile suddenly stopped.

Meanwhile Pinochet had gingerly allowed trade unions to reorganise themselves under pressure from the International Labour Office and the US labour confederation AFL-CIO. Provided that they did not aspire to raise wage levels at such a difficult time they were allowed greater latitude than in previous years.

One of their leaders was Tucapel Jiménez, a veteran anti-communist who had supported Pinochet's coup. He had got himself a bad name with the CNI as 'a stone in the government's shoe' because of his continuing commitment to maintaining workers' wage rates and was trying to organise a national strike for March 1982. The copper miners, the aristocrats of the Chilean working class, were restive and teachers in schools and universities were seeking to improve their wages. Socialists, Communists and Christian Democrats were beginning to come together in a tentative union federation.

On the sunny summer morning of 25 February 1982 Jiménez was flagged down on the outskirts of Santiago by three men. They shot him five times in the neck using weapons from the CNI armoury and then cut his windpipe. There was no general strike. The supposed assassin, a carpenter, was later found with both his wrists slashed in what was said to be a suicide. (In September 1999 General Humberto Gordon was put in detention at a Santiago military hospital after a judge charged him with abetting the premeditated murder of Tucapel Jiménez.)

Pinochet's ministers had to spend $3 billion on rescuing the banks which had lent to business now unable to repay the loans they had received. In January 1983 alone the Banco de Chile, the Banco de

Santiago, the Banco Internacional, the Banco Concepción, the Banco Unido de Fomento and the Colocadora Nacional de Valores all had to be taken over from bankers who were enthusiastic for Pinochet but whose balance sheets were showing they had been failed to run their businesses prudently. The lack of financial ability in the government meant that Pinochet's ministers had to ask the UN International Monetary Fund for a loan of nearly 800 million Special Drawing Rights, the emergency funds available for IMF signatory countries. The UN's other financial agency, the World Bank, said the following year half Chile's production structure was bankrupt and the largest banks were bust.

The General's dreams were in ruins. Between 1940 and 1973, the year of his coup, the Chilean economy had grown at the rate of about 4 per cent per year. Between 1974 and 1985 the growth rate was no more than 1.7 per cent. In 1985 Chileans were on average no richer than they were when Pinochet took over.

However, a new generation of super-rich Chileans had been spawned amid the stagnation and poverty that the majority experienced. There were more yet to be created as Chile began to recover from the debacle and move into a period of much faster economic growth. In the 1980s the world economy moved out of recession and revenues from copper exports bounded upwards. Inflation calmed, the number of unemployed fell and the rate of growth of the gross national product hovered around the 10 per cent per annum. As boom time returned – particularly for the rich – Pinochet's friends at home and abroad proclaimed a Chilean economic miracle.

Perhaps the simplest way of becoming super-rich in Chile was to buy state-owned companies that the state was selling off at rock-bottom prices. Most of these were concentrated in the management of a holding company CORFO, the national development corporation. Founded in 1939 during the left-wing government of President Pedro Aguirre Cerda, it was preserved and added to by successive governments of all persuasions. Allende in particular used it as a home for the companies he nationalised; during his term in office the number of CORFO firms rose from 46 in 1970 to some 300 in 1973. Twelve years later their number had shrunk back to 24.

The results of the late 1980s boom could be seen in the landscape of the capital. In particular, the eastern areas of the city were transformed. Shining new bank and office buildings went up beside new landmarks such as the Hyatt hotel and Alto Las Condes, a sparkling new shopping mall. By the time the UN World Bank issued its annual report for 1991 it was full of praise for Pinochet's Chile, and named it as one of the group of countries 'with a record of sustained reform'. 'Chile is the most advanced country in this group, having been one of the first to start the process,' the Bank concluded. 'It has had a steady growth for the past six years, and the investment rate is now at an historical peak.'

At the other end of the city from the Hyatt hotel the soup kitchens had disappeared. Chilean society had become inexorably divided. That process continued to such an extent that at the beginning of 1999 the UN Economic Commission for Latin America and the Caribbean – always a sounder guide to the realities of Latin America than its sister organisation the UN World Bank – reported the gap between rich and poor in Chile had grown so wide that it rivalled that of Brazil, which had been for years the country with the worst income inequality in Latin America.

In the midst of this prosperity repression and torture of the most violent nature continued until the very end of the dictatorship. The claims made by a politically active 17 year-old girl, whom we will call Soledad, revealed the character of repression in the late 1980s.

According to her sworn statement to lawyers in London, Soledad was seized and bundled into a car at 9pm one night as she left work by a group of men whom she presumed to be from the CNI. She was manacled and taken to a building which she presumed to be a torture centre. She was forced inside and given a heavy blow on the top of the head which rendered her unconscious. When she came to she found herself naked with a large gash on her head and strapped hand and foot to something which resembled a dentist's chair. Then began an interrogation about her political activities and her associates which, she reckoned, lasted for up to 36 hours.

She was taken to an adjoining room by two women who tied her spread-eagled to a bedstead, a pillow put under her buttocks. A rod some 30 cms long like a cattle prod tube was placed in her vagina and a strong electric current was applied. The interrogation continued. She was then raped. She was then thrown on a bed where three people inflicted the most grievous sexual attack on her.

Sometime later the first man raped her again and repeated demands that she should identify people in a set of photographs. When she would not she was left alone naked in a bare room where she was served three successive meals. As the room did not contain even a bucket she was obliged to urinate on the floor.

After a third rape, she was taken off in a car and driven past her house. Later the car halted and Soledad was seized by the hair and flung to the side of the road. She survived but, as happens to all victims of torture, carries the marks of her ordeal branded into her memory.

By the late 1980s Chile had indeed 'a record of sustained reform'. But there were still no indications that the state would desist from arbitrary kidnapping, detention, torture and assassination.

In the lexicon of the international funding institutions like the IMF and the UN World Bank, however, Chile was an overachiever, the Latin American darling of the international investment structure. At the end of the nineties Chile has become, for its middle and upper-class citizens, a consumer's paradise.

In the New Chile 92 percent of citizens have a television set. At the weekends in the glossy Santiago shopping malls families stroll from shop to shop, looking at microwaves and videocassette recorders, some voyeuristically, some with the genuine possibility of buying. The traditional, unostenatious Chile has gone. 'In comparison, today to live luxuriously is a sign of prestige,' writes sociologist Tomás Moulian in his book *Chile Today: Anatomy of a Myth*. 'The car that costs fifty thousand dollars is exhibited as a decoration of heroic mercantilism, an intelligent gain in a competitive market. It's necessary to have a large house if you want to be someone on the ladder of success. It's indispensable to wear fashionable clothes. To be rich it is necessary to see yourself with other rich people. Wealth is not private, rather it is exhibited. To hide it would be bad taste.'

Family fortunes, family adventures

'I'm the general of the poor'
Augusto Pinochet, 1982

The Pinochet family is a large one. By 1999 the General's five children and their various spouses had given him twenty-five grandchildren and four great-grand children. Among those who benefited most from Pinochet's privatisation process and business deals with the armed forces – whose budget was always buoyant – was the Pinochet family itself.

Pinochet's wife Lucía claimed that her and her husband's only wealth was his army pension. This claim is difficult to square with the facts. Indeed, the truth about the millions controlled by this family was kept a secret for a long time – at times, as we shall see, by recourse to threats of military violence.

As part of the deal under which Pinochet surrendered the presidency in 1990, the army forced an agreement that no government decisions taken before that date would be examined or called into question. As time has gone by, and particularly since Pinochet's arrest, interest has increased about the manner in which a man whose salary, exclusive of house, domestic staff, chauffeur and bodyguards, was by European or US standards, ridiculously small.

In his book *Para entender a los militares*, Raúl Sohr, the doyen of Chilean commentators on military affairs, gives the official remuneration table of the air force in September 1988. Its commander-in-chief was earning 329,925 Chilean pesos per month, after deductions of 46,403 pesos for pension contributions. That represented £838.12p (US$1,341) per month or £10,057 (US$16,092) per year. The book suggests the sum earned by the commander-in-chief of the army would not have been substantially different.

Throughout his dictatorship Pinochet had made much of his admiration for and practice of thrift. But it is difficult to see how even the thriftiest officer solely dependent on a salary of such a size could have amassed the sums which he was later to command.

In April 1999 the Chilean magazine *Punto Final*, using work published in the 22 March edition of the Mexico City daily *El*

RIGGS

```
        AUGUSTO PINOCHET UGARTE &/OR                          0
        LUCIA HIRIART DE PINOCHET
        HOLD MAIL
        C/O RHB-IPBD
        MAIL CODE 8-9002
```

76-750-393   PAGE   1

STATEMENT PERIOD 03-01-97   THROUGH 03-31-97

MONEY MARKET SUMMARY

OPENING BALANCE	1,169,308.23	ACCOUNT #	16 750 393
+DEPOSITS	12,465.75	# OF ENCLOSURES	0
+INTEREST	3,907.00	AVERAGE BALANCE	1,800,038.51
-CHECKS AND DEBITS	1,000,000.00	INTEREST PAID YTD	6,866.48
-NEW BALANCE	175,690.98		

MONEY MARKET ACTIVITY

DEPOSITS	DATE	AMOUNT	DEPOSITS	DATE	AMOUNT
REF 01	03-27	12,465.75	REF 02	03-31	3,907.00

CHECKS	DATE	AMOUNT	CHECKS	DATE	AMOUNT
REF 03	03-27	1,000,000.00			

REFERENCE DESCRIPTION

REF 01 INT. TRANSFER CREDIT FROM CD NO. 00-284-188
REF 02 INTEREST CREDIT
REF 03 DEBIT MEMO

MONEY MARKET BALANCES

02-28	1,159,318.23	03-27	171,783.98	03-31	175,690.98

MONEY MARKET INTEREST

FROM	THROUGH	NO DAYS	RATE	AVG COLECTED BALANCE
03-01-97	03-31-97	31	4.600000	$1,000,038.51

ANNUAL PERCENTAGE YIELD EARNED   4.69%

FOR PERSONAL ACCOUNT INQUIRIES, CALL (301) 887-6000. OUTSIDE
METROPOLITAN WASHINGTON, DC, CALL 1(800) 368-5800. FOR CORPORATE
ACCOUNT INQUIRIES, CALL (301) 887-6530. FOR INQUIRIES ON ELECTRONIC
TRANSACTIONS, CALL (301) 887-CARD.

Universal, published details of account number 16 750 393 at the Riggs Bank of Washington DC in the name of the General and his wife for the period between 1 and 31 March 1997.

The bank statement reveals large cash movements. It itemised an opening balance of US$1,169,308.23, deposits during the month of US$12,465.75 and interest paid by the bank of US$3,907.00. A cheque paid on 27 March reduced the balance at the end of the month to US$175,690.98.

In his book *La Familia Militar*, the veteran Chilean journalist Hernán Millas itemised the General's real estate. First there was a large house in La Dehesa, a fashionable area on the outskirts of the capital. In 1996 he bought a holiday house at Iquique. There followed an apartment at the seaside resort of Reñaca which he bought in 1998 at a cost the Chilean daily *El Mercurio* estimated at 198 million pesos. His property also includes an office with a parking facilities in the centre of Valparaiso.

Pinochet's wife Lucía appeared to have a steady source of funds as head of CEMA-Chile, an umbrella organisation founded in 1964 by the wife of President Eduardo Frei to bring together the country's various members of the nation mothers' union. The scheme was continued by Allende's wife. After the coup the individual centres came under military control. When Pinochet was named head of state in 1974 Lucía took over the presidency of CEMA which she re-baptised CEMA-Chile, turning it into a foundation. She received a substantial amount to cover her expenses.

The dictatorship decreed that CEMA-Chile should receive a substantial contribution from the football lottery Polla Chilena de Beneficencia. Though the present activities of CEMA-Chile are principally confined to the care of families of non-commissioned officers of the armed forces, it is the recipient of the largest single annual contribution from the Polla. According to Millas, in 1998 it received 148 million pesos. (The investigation also revealed that something called the September Foundation also receives a substantial sum from the Polla. Millas was unable to learn of its organisation and function).

In April 1993 the Council for the Defence of the State, the CDE, a senior constitutional body in Santiago, called for an investigation of possible fraud against the state in the case of the sale of a rifle factory, SIG Valmoval, a Chilean affiliate of the Swiss company, to the Chilean army in late 1989. The investigation threw up a well-known name: Augusto Pinochet Junior.

Pinochet's eldest son had started with a career in the army, reaching the rank of captain. He was then given a job with the Central Bank of Chile in New York. According to *Los Hijos de Pinochet*, a study of the enrichment of those around Pinochet published in Santiago in 1995 by Víctor Osorio and Iván Cabezas, Augusto apparently acted as middle man, heading a company called PSP which bought SIG Valmoval and sold it on to the army commanded by his father.

The Council for the Defence of the State pointed to evidence, forwarded to it by the Chamber of Deputies in 1991, that Augusto had received three cheques to the value of 971.9 million pesos, nearly £2 million. This was the beginning of an affair which became known at the Pinocheques.

A month after the investigation was put in motion, the army, under General Pinochet's orders, threatened violence in the streets. On 22 May 1993 the Santiago daily *La Nación* carried the headline 'Case of the cheques of Pinochet's son reopened'. There was an immediate reaction from the army under Pinochet's command. President Aylwin was on a visit to Scandinavia and authority lay in the hands of the acting head of state Enrique Krauss. General Ballerino was sent to Krauss to tell him that the army high command was incandescent with rage and would not allow Judge Alejandro Solís, whom they considered a left-winger, to hear the Pinocheques case. Pinochet ordered a grade one military alert and the mobilisation of the First Division.

In his book Ascanio Cavallo, *La Historia Oculta de la Transición* tells of how the military discussed mobilising tanks outside the Moneda, of dismissing the Congress as had been done in 1973, this time calling new elections. In June 1993 the judge assigned to the case declared it was beyond his jurisdiction. Shortly afterwards he was promoted to the Appeal Court.

In 1994 the General was ordered to testify in Santiago in connection with the sale of SIG Valmoval, which he refused to do. The investigation was called off in June 1995 after a direct appeal to the CDE by President Eduardo Frei, despite the fact that nine of the twelve members of the CDE had voted in favour of the dictator's prosecution for fraud. Observers decided that Frei's act of indulgence seemed to be part of a political deal between the army and the civilian government.

One of the first accounts of the Pinochet family's prospering fortunes was written by me in *The Observer* of 4 July 1983 and was not denied. It made reference to a Chilean businessman, Julio Ponce, then the husband of Pinochet's daughter Verónica. Ponce was widely known in Chilean business circles as *El Yerno*, (the Son-in-law) or even *El Yernísimo*, (the Super Son-in-law). In the years after the coup Ponce acquired a number of high offices in various companies: Conaf, Celuluosa Arauco Constitución, Compañía de Teléfonos, Chilectra, Complejo Maderero Panguipulli. Many of these were state property later to be privatised.

In the early 1980s Ponce found himself vice-president of CORFO. But in July 1983, as I reported at the time, CORFO announced he had quit 'for personal reasons'. He denied that version, but said that only his father-in-law was allowed to reveal the real reasons. He had been accused of using CORFO land and employees on his own cattle-raising business in the south of Chile.

The privatisation process from 1973 onward had boosted the Pinochets' assets through SOQUIMICH, the largest Chilean producer of iodine and nitrate fertiliser. Originally a CORFO company, after privatisation in the mid-1970s it was presided over by Ponce. In 1998 its profit, according to Millas, came to US$67 million.

The successive husbands of Pinochet's elder daughter Lucía have also attracted controversy. The first, a veterinary surgeon, rose from attending to the needs of animals to a senior position in the state-controlled television sector in the years immediately after the coup. The second, Jorge Aravena, was in the insurance business and a director of an insurance agency, Metrópoli. The Santiago weekly magazine *Hoy* reported that Metrópoli had taken the equivalent of some £500,000 in commissions from the Instituto de Seguros del Estado, ISE, the broker for most of the state-owned corporations. There was some questioning about why ISE, given its strong position in the market, needed a broker at all, whether related to the ruling family or not. The vice-president of ISE was for a time Colonel Mario Gutiérrez, a cousin of General Pinochet.

With Pinochet out of the way indefinitely due to his arrest in Britain in October 1998, many of those in Chile seeking investigation of his affairs were encouraged to take their inquiries further. Quoting Switzerland's flourishing trade with Chile, Professor Jean Ziegler, a leading Socialist MP from Geneva and a long-standing critic of the country's tradition of extreme banking secrecy, called in 1998 for the seizure in short order of what he termed 'large private bank accounts in Switzerland belonging to some Chilean generals, notably Augusto Pinochet, at the time the commander-in-chief of the army'. The Swiss Socialist Party, a member of the ruling coalition in Berne, sought an official investigation of the Pinochet arms-dealing and financial activities, as was reported in the *Tribune de Genève* newspaper.

The party did this in the realisation that the Swiss government had the authority to seize Pinochet property under Article 102 of the constitution which in the past had allowed the Swiss government to sequester the assets of Ferdinand Marcos and the Duvalier family of Haiti.

Chile's relations with the Swiss government had already been very strained; Switzerland was in the queue behind Spain to have the former Chilean dictator extradited from Britain to face trial in Geneva on charges of the kidnapping and murder of a Swiss citizen, Alexei Jacquard. In September 1998, amid much official Chilean indignation, Switzerland rejected a Chilean demand for the extradition of Patricio Ortiz, an anti-Pinochet activist imprisoned by a military tribunal in 1995 who escaped and fled to Switzerland last year.

Inquiries by the Swiss authorities drew attention to Augusto Junior's dealings with two Swiss companies which supplied equipment to the Chilean forces. MOWAG built military vehicles and SIG manufactured light automatic weapons. But in Chile there was reluctance to follow up the Swiss investigation. 'We don't dare touch the story here. It'd be more than our lives are worth,' remarked a senior Chilean journalist, conscious of the continuing powers of the armed forces that President Eduardo Frei Ruiz-Tagle has been unable to tame.

No one in the Pinochet family has been convicted of any financial irregularity, at least not under the laws of Chile as they are were inherited from the time of Augusto Pinochet's dictatorship and as they are at present interpreted.

The Pinochet children have meanwhile been the subject of much comment in Chile. In some cases the interest has centred on their divorces and on in some cases on reported tendencies towards violence. The divorces did not appear to have worried the Chilean church unduly. Unyielding in its stand against divorce for others, the Vatican moved rapidly to relieve the Pinochet children of any matrimonial embarrassment.

Hernán Millas, author *of La Familia Militar*, which contains much information about the Pinochets, recounts how the youngest daughter, Jacqueline, had her first marriage solemnised by Raúl Hasbún, the well-known right-wing cleric who had gained a great reputation attacking the Allende government on television. Four children were born of that union before it ended. Another marriage took place, this time a civil affair, during which a fifth child arrived. Jacqueline's third marriage was also performed by Hasbún. The Vatican had been persuaded to annul the first marriage and to admit to the fact that it had not recognised the validity of the second. This enabled the ineffable priest to administer the sacrament once again.

There was little public fuss – Chilean journalists knew the consequences of making a fuss – over another family matter which bore striking similarities to the 1969 Chappaquiddick case involving Senator Edward Kennedy and the death of Mary Jo Kopechne, who had been a passenger in his car.

Some ten years later, as Millas recounts in his book, Marco Antonio, Pinochet's youngest son, was involved in a car accident one wet night outside the Las Condes cinema in a smart part of Santiago. His passenger was Natalicia Ducci, the daughter of a respected professional. Both, according to Hernán Millas, had been to a party from where Natalicia's father had arranged to pick her up after she telephoned to ask him to collect her. Marco Antonio however persuaded her to allow him to take her home. After the car crashed the young man's bodyguards took him and the car away. Natalicia's body was found by her distraught parents some hours later, where she had drowned in a gutter. The bodyguards had devoted themselves to driver. The girl was left to die. There was of course no charge ever made against the dictator's son.

A negotiated retreat

The rules that Pinochet had dictated in the Constitution of 1980 gave him power that no elected politician could challenge. According to the terms of the Constitution, a wholesale amnesty for the crimes committed by the dictatorship in the years before 1978 was granted; the armed forces were guaranteed ten per cent of the sum earned from sales by Codelco, the state copper corporation; Pinochet continued as commander-in-chief of the army and could not be removed; the military continued to have to answer only to military courts and not civilian ones.

The Chilean Congress was set up with a system of rules which, if they were obeyed, prevented any alteration to the constitution, and the senators appointed by Pinochet were given the effective power of veto over constitutional amendments. Heavy punishment was decreed for anyone who was found guilty of insulting the armed forces.

On 11 March 1990, Patricio Aylwin waited at the presidential residence at Cerro Castillo overlooking Valparaiso to receive Pinochet, who was coming to congratulate him on his electoral victory. The new president must have been conscious of how tightly the general had pinioned him politically.

Throughout the next eight years, Pinochet was to make it clear to Aylwin and, eventually to Aylwin's successor and fellow Christian Democrat Eduardo Frei Ruiz-Tagle, son of the former president, that what a civilian defence minister might think about what the army was of little interest or concern to the man who remained its commander-in-chief.

The first working encounter between the new president and the old army commander-in-chief on 13 May 1990 was chilly. A small crowd was on hand to boo Pinochet. No less frigid was the struggle over the parking spaces in the Moneda car park. Pinochet's vehicles had arrived early and occupied the spaces reserved for the new civilian incumbents. Carlos Bascuñán, Aylwin's chief of staff, told Colonel Lepe, the commander of Pinochet's escort, that the next time he arrived he would have to ask permission to park.

The politicians and their staff attempted to arrive at a balanced view of the violations of human rights during Pinochet's regime. Within days of assuming the presidency Aylwin established the

National Truth and Reconciliation Commission to investigate the most serious human rights violations. As its president Aylwin chose Raúl Rettig, the aged former Radical senator with whom Allende had fought a duel in 1952, probably over a woman. Neither having been killed in that encounter, Rettig was later gratefully to accept Allende's gracious offer of the ambassadorship in Brazil.

But Pinochet quickly demonstrated that whatever Rettig's findings, no one in the army was to be allowed to express any regrets for the murder and torture, despite the fact that 70,000 people crowded to cheer the President's decision in the National Stadium, the very place where so many abuses and summary executions had taken place.

September 1990 was a particularly bad month for the General. On the fourth day of the month the remains of Salvador Allende were given a state funeral in the capital's central cemetery. Two days later more than fifty members of the Chamber of Deputies signed a motion to set up a committee to investigate Augusto Junior and his Pinocheques. In December Pinochet threatened military violence over the committee. He succeeded in intimidating the government for the moment, but did not finally do away with the matter.

Pinochet attempted to do the same thing again in 1993, this time under Aylwin's successor Eduardo Frei. The Pinocheques question had to be filed away once more, this time at the express requirement of the elected head of state, conscious of what Pinochet could do with his troops against anyone brave enough to investigate the financial matters of his family. Commenting on the political effectiveness of the general's bullying tactics, Cavallo comments, 'Starting from the case of the pinocheques he obtained results which not even the most ambitious strategist could have imagined'.

And all the time the dead were rising from the earth. In June 1990 nineteen bodies were discovered at Pisagua. Forensic scientists established they had been buried just after the coup; in August ten more were discovered at Paine; in June 1991 there was a new court case about the twenty-six corpses found at Calama; in September 127 were exhumed from plot 29 at the Santiago General Cemetery. In 1995, on a lonely beach in Uruguay, the remains of Eugenio Berríos, the DINA's 'mad scientist' appeared, mushrooming from the shifting sands.

There remained one thorny issue where Pinochet was vulnerable, the case of his friend and colleague Manuel Contreras. The US government had been faced with a problem by the bold Chilean action in killing Letelier in the centre of Washington. Pinochet was an ideological ally who might not have come to power without its help. The intelligence services of the two nations were deeply involved with each other. Yet it would have been difficult to completely overlook the murder. The decision therefore was made to handle it in the most diplomatic way possible, going after the minor actors and attempting to deflect attention from Pinochet himself.

The general understood the tactic. He had acquiesced when Washington called for several suspects to be extradited to face charges in the US. After some legal jousting in April 1978, Michael Townley was whisked off to Pudahuel, handcuffed, with only the clothes he wore. Two US officials received him as he was put aboard an Ecuatoriana flight which left Santiago for Quito and New York. As he took his seat he burst into tears. Once in Washington he bargained successfully for a light sentence, agreeing to plead guilty to a minor charge. In exchange for his information he received a light sentence and on release was given a new identity as part of the FBI's witness protection program. In January 1979, in a district court not far from the White House in Washington, the trial of three Cubans for their part in Letelier's murder began. Two months later they too were sentenced. Successive US governments sought the extradition of Manuel Contreras but did so in ways they knew would be unsuccessful. After some argument Contreras was retired from the army with honour.

But Letelier's sister Fabiola, his son Juan Pablo, who was to become a deputy in Congress, and many of his friends were unwilling to let the matter rest. In May 1995, after much manoeuvring, Pinochet had to bow to the inevitable and surrender Contreras to the Chilean law.

At the time Contreras had fallen on comparatively hard times. He was living in the south of Chile and working the rather unproductive Viejo Roble, 'Old Oak' farm, near Puerto Montt. Separated from his wife Mara Teresa, he was living with his former secretary, Nélida. As the day for the final decision on a sentence approached Pinochet sent a Brigadier General Eugenio Videla down to the farm. In his book *La Historia Oculta de la Transición* Ascanio Cavallo quotes Videla as saying, 'General, on the instructions of the minister and my General Pinochet, I have come to propose to you that you go either to Easter Island or Chaitén'; the choice being between being lost in the Pacific or being lost in a tiny township of 3,000 people in Chile's deep south. Contreras replied that he would not flee like a guilty man, nor would he accept to go to prison.

On 30 May 1995 Judge Adolfo Bañados sentenced Contreras to seven years imprisonment for the killing of Letelier and gave six to his former second-in-command Brigadier Pedro Espinoza. Even worse for the commander-in-chief – and a sign of the times – Bañados was a civilian judge. Hitherto the military had refused to appear before non-military judges. There was a delay while Contreras pleaded illness, but by October he was behind bars, albeit it a new and relatively luxurious establishment at Punta Peuco. By the time Contreras settled himself into his airy cell a court in Rome had sentenced him in absentia to twenty years' imprisonment for the attack on Bernardo Leighton and his wife all those years ago.

The intimate relationship lasting decades between Pinochet and Contreras was finally shattered. Though he did not share their ultimate fate, he joined a long list of those betrayed by Augusto Pinochet: Allende, Tohá, the Prats, the Leightons, Lutz, Bonilla, to name but a few. In February 1998 in his statement to the Supreme Court Contreras was to have his small taste of vengeance.

Meanwhile in December 1993 a second civilian president, like Aylwin a Christian Democrat, was elected. Eduardo Frei Ruiz-Tagle, whose father had ruled from 1964 till the day he unwillingly passed the sash of office to Salvador Allende in 1970, won 58 per cent of the 7.3 million votes cast. The Communist Party (whose dominance both Pinochet and Kissinger had said they still feared) won less than 5 per cent of the vote, not enough to give them even a single seat in either house of Congress, the Senate or the House of Representatives.

Frei Ruiz-Tagle was to remain as frightened of Pinochet as Aylwin had been – perhaps more. For fear of what Pinochet could do as head of the army he ordered the closure of the investigation being carried out by the Council for the Defence of the State on the question of the Pinocheques. He appeared content to allow Pinochet to continue exercising authority over the armed forces which no other government would have allowed. Neither civilian president was able to undo the legal framework of the constitution Pinochet constructed for himself. In *Carta Abierta a Patricio Aylwin*, a book he published in 1998, Armando Uribe, the former Chilean ambassador in Peking, chided the civilian politicians for their lack of courage. He wrote, 'What we have today is not an imperfect democracy; rather is it an imperfect dictatorship.'

On 10 March 1998 at the Military School Pinochet's flag with the five stars was lowered for the last time and handed to him by an orderly. The old dictator's eyes filled with tears as the command of the army passed to his successor General Ricardo Izurieta. All that remained for him to do was to take up the position he had created for himself, Senator for Life. That ceremony in the new congress building built in Valparaiso, the city to which Pinochet had imperiously exiled it, was a rowdy one with left-wing members marching up and down across the floor of the Senate with placards in their hands. As citizens rioted outside, 500 people were arrested and 34 injured. Inside in his senatorial seat Pinochet grinned. He had fixed his own immunity, he had presided over the enrichment of himself and his family and he had a position which he could occupy till he died. He had transformed the face of Chile. More to the point, people, above all the politicians he despised, still feared him. Never was more apposite the quotation from Cicero's first Philippic: *Oderint dum metuant*, 'Let them hate provided that they fear'.

On that bright evening in 1998 a long and sunny retirement beckoned.

V

Nemesis

'The Pinochet case became the most important test case for
international law since Nuremberg itself'
Geoffrey Robertson QC, in his book *Crimes against Humanity*

The globalisation of guilt

'I don't trust anyone'
Augusto Pinochet, April 1986

The general's nemesis came in the form of a bespectacled Spanish
judge, Baltasar Garzón. Born into a middle-class family in the
province of Jaén, in his youth Garzón seemed attracted to the catholic
priesthood. He also enjoyed flamenco and pop music and in his
last year at school developed a passion for the girl whom he would
later marry. Casting thoughts of priesthood aside, he worked at a
petrol station to supplement his income as he studied law.

A few years after graduation he was appointed to the Audiencia
Nacional, the highest tribunal for criminal cases in Spain, at the
very young age of 32. There he rapidly gained nation-wide attention
as the judge who was not afraid to prosecute drug mafias and other
high-profile targets.

Garzón, it seems, was always a hands-on prosecutor: on one
occasion in June 1990 he sat in a helicopter and personally directed
350 police officers on a raid as part of an anti-drug campaign in
Galicia, the region of Spain where narcotics are smuggled ashore
from passing ships. He then turned his attention to the widespread
corruption which accompanied Expo Sevilla, the world fair which
took place in the Andalusian capital in 1992.

With Garzón's high profile came the need for a constant
bodyguard. Garzón, popularly known as 'Superjudge', caught the
attention of the Socialist prime minister, Felipe González, who
persuaded him to stand for parliament as an independent in Madrid.

He accepted the suggestion and in elections in 1993 polled almost as many votes as González himself. González put him in charge of the National Drugs Plan.

However, before long Garzón expressed his disgust at the corruption he saw in government circles and the lack of official support for his initiatives. He joined with a parliamentary colleague and threatened to vote for the opposition if González did not take action against bribery and the misuse of funds. He returned to the judiciary as head of the Fifth Court of the Audiencia Nacional, and brought charges against a number of very senior figures including the former secretary of state for security and his secretary, the former Bilbao police chief and the former general secretary of the Basque socialists. Worse, at least for González, he uncovered evidence that the Spanish police had tortured Basque separatists. The case did much to encompass González' eventual defeat at the polls in March 1996.

Garzón was not always successful. He pursued Monzer al-Kassar, the Syrian drugs and arms dealer based in southern Spain who was implicated in the Chilean arms trade. Al-Kassar had previously operated from London where in 1977 he had been sentenced to two and a half years in jail for conspiracy to import narcotics. In 1992 Garzón had him imprisoned on remand on charges of involvement in the hijacking of the Italian liner the *Achille Lauro* in which an elderly American man was killed. The case was thrown out, not least because one of the principal witnesses for the prosecution had fallen to his death from a fourth floor window.

Al-Kassar went back to a life of gaudy luxury in his palace at Marbella on Spain's Costa del Sol, where the table linen was embroidered with gold and servants ran to the master's service at the click of his fingers. (In 1999 al-Kassar's Madrid lawyer Ernesto Díaz-Bastien was involved in the defence of Pinochet, submitting a two-page deposition to the British court arguing that Spain had no authority to prosecute the Chilean general. Speaking to the author from Damascus in June 1999, al-Kassar asked who Pinochet was and denied that Díaz-Bastien had submitted the deposition in Pinochet's favour at his behest. However some months earlier he had been overheard boasting in private that he would finance Pinochet's defence.)

In 1996 Garzón's attention turned for the first time to Latin America. He became interested in the case of the atrocities committed against Spanish citizens in Argentina during the military regime which seized power in 1976. There was a mass of evidence to hand about one of the cruellest and most discreditable periods in Latin American history. The leaders of this supposedly Christian country had indulged in the most horrific practices. The Argentine Navy had turned its Navy Mechanical School into its principal torture centre, where naval officers increased the fortunes they amassed from administrative corruption by selling babies born to their female prisoners to childless couples. One officer, Francisco Scilingo, motivated not by remorse but by a grudge about promotion, revealed to the distinguished Argentine journalist, Horacio Verbitsky, the details about the flights, regularly scheduled for Wednesdays, during which political dissidents, bound, naked and, if they were lucky, drugged, were thrown out of the plane into the South Atlantic Ocean. Garzón investigated 320 cases involving Spanish citizens, and demanded the arrest of senior Argentine officers, including Scilingo. Later these atrocities were found to be copies of similar actions in Chile in 1973.

Initially the fate of Spaniards murdered or kidnapped in Chile was not Garzón's concern but that of a fellow judge, Manuel García Castellón. More cautious and politically conservative than Garzón, García Castellón, was head of the Sixth Court of the Audiencia Nacional. His investigation of Pinochet was supported by a resolution of the European Parliament in September 1997 and in January 1998 he spent a week in Washington seeking evidence against Pinochet from US officials and witnesses living in the US. In mid-1998 the two Spanish judges reached an amicable decision that Garzón should take over Spanish concerns about atrocities in both Argentina and Chile.

Meanwhile the case against Pinochet was being prepared by a Spaniard who had been close to Salvador Allende during his presidency indeed he had been in the presidential palace on the day of his death.

Juan Garcés was born in the province of Valencia in 1944. In his twenties he received a doctorate in political science at the Sorbonne and left shortly after for Santiago, attracted by the prospect of working with a government which was attempting radically to change society.

After Allende's death he wrote several powerful books about Chile. *Allende et l'Experience chilienne* was printed in French, Spanish, Portuguese, Italian and Japanese editions while *Orlando Letelier, Testimonio y vindicación*, which Garcés wrote in collaboration with the American writer Saul Landau, was the most authoritative study of the assassination.

Garcés' experience in Europe and Latin America and subsequently in the service of the United Nations was supplemented by the several years he spent after the coup at the Institute for Policy Studies in Washington, where Letelier had also worked. Together Garzón and Garcés painstakingly prepared the trap which was sprung for Pinochet on the night of 16 October.

Pinochet's arrest exploded a bombshell in the usually quiet groves of international law. The consequences were almost uniformly positive. An important precedent had been set to the effect that governments' practice, long adhered to by successive British and other governments, of ignoring the terms of the international conventions against torture and refraining from detaining those suspected of such crimes, could not continue. It also improved prospects for the establishment of an International Criminal Court. Pinochet's arrest was a strong indication that the process of globalisation, for so long confined to questions of international trade, the internet and the freedom of multinational companies to strike down barriers to their global activity, was about to be extended to other areas of life.

The case against Pinochet, backed up by the efforts of the Letelier, Horman and Moffitt families certainly prompted the Clinton administration to start publishing many of the closed files on US-Chilean relations, shedding light on events that many in the US had hoped would be kept secret. The arrest of Pinochet was a powerful boost to the decades of effort by the Letelier, Horman and Moffitt families to seek justice for the murder of their loved ones.

The first 5,800 of these released documents confirmed what many on the inside had suspected for years: that the US authorities knew of the widespread campaign of torture and murder and of Operation Condor. Its diplomats in Santiago put the most optimistic construction on what information they had to their superiors in

Washington, and the US chose to minimise to the outside world the effects of the reign of terror.

It therefore came as no surprise when, at the beginning of July 1999, after the publication of the first documents that Saul Landau, a US writer concerned with the murder of Letelier, called for the consideration of charges being filed against former President Bush and Dr Kissinger for having 'willingly abetted mass murder and torture'.

The detention of such a man as Pinochet put tyrants and their auxiliaries around the world under notice that they could no longer flout international law and expect impunity outside their own countries. The principle of universal jurisdiction – much scorned by conservatives – and the duty of governments to apprehend those suspected of committing them were strengthened by the Pinochet affair.

Loud calls came, for instance, from the anti-Castro lobbies in Florida for the arrest of Fidel Castro. There was even a wild suggestion from time to time that the Queen of England should be detained for the supposed crimes committed in her name during the 1982 Falklands War. In August 1999 in Argentina a judge gave leave to a plaintiff who had lost family members during that country's dirty war to sue Admiral Massera, the commander of the Argentine navy and the architect of some of the worst excesses during the military dictatorship.

In Chile, the noose was being tightened around some of Pinochet's closest associates. In June 1999 the Chilean government issued a list of 38 people whom it cautioned against travelling abroad. The list included Generals Leigh, Benavides, Matthei, Carrasco, Sinclair, Stange, Torres, and Baeza. It further included several of those who took part in the Caravan of Death: Arellano himself and Colonels Sergio Arredondo and Marcelo Manuel Moren, alias 'El Ronco'. The successive chiefs of the DINA/CNI, Generals Contreras, Mena Gordon and Salas Wenzel were there, as were Mónica Madariaga, Pinochet's cousin, and Major Corbalán, the man with the narcotic connections. Though his name did not figure on the list, General Jorge Ballerino, a former aide-de-camp to Pinochet, decided not to attend a conference in Warsaw in May 1999, according to the Madrid daily *El País*.

A change came over the judiciary in 1999 as several dozen serious charges from individuals relating to human rights violations during the dictatorship were allowed to be formally registered against Pinochet, a state of affairs which would previously have been unthinkable. Members of the general public were losing their fear of reprisals from Pinochet's supporters. It also suggested that the judiciary itself, which had for so long treated Pinochet and his associates with obsequiousness, was realising that such an attitude was no longer tenable.

Nevertheless in the general's homeland lights still burned for him. The wealth of the Pinochet family did not stop sophisticated techniques being employed after the General's arrest to collect more money for him. Among the rich and middle class of Santiago a hard-selling Marathon campaign to collect funds for Chile's former dictator was set up. Known as the 'Pinochethon', it was run with considerable sophistication by Alfonso Márquez de la Plata Yrarrázabal, at 65 years old one of the longest-serving ministers in the dictator's different cabinets, from his luxury flat nine floors up overlooking the Avenida Kennedy Golf Club.

One of its most successful gambits, as he boasted in 1999 in the Chilean press, was a computerised cold canvass by telephone. A recorded message invited telephone subscribers to say whether they support Pinochet or not. If the answer was 'yes' – many feared to give any different answer – then they were invited to dial in a number, from 2,000 to 20,000. That figure in pesos (between £4 and £40) was collected via the phone bill. In the case of larger amounts a messenger was sent round to collect a cheque. In the first days of the campaign, Márquez said, 223,000 calls were made.

'One Saturday someone donated a million pesos, £20,000', Pinochet's fund-raiser said. 'He has no fortune but he does have friends.' In an interview with the pro-Pinochet newspaper *El Mercurio* he claimed that Pinochet's property was limited to his house in La Dehesa and small farm at El Melocotón, both situated between the city centre and the Andes.

Meanwhile, Augusto Junior went to Miami at the beginning of 1999 to collect money independently. This was, he said, to be devoted to his father's expenses. An official announcement was made in Santiago that he was doing it without the authorisation of the General.

The lawyers dealing with the extradition case in Madrid also obtained unexpected benefits from the Pinochet affair, this time in international business affairs.

The revelation of the conduct of the dictator from 1973 to 1990 brought a growing acknowledgement around the globe that, as well as crimes against people, great irregularities concerning property had been committed in Chile during the Pinochet regime. The illegal expropriation in 1976 of the property of his opponents was brought into contention in 1999. The case centred around the newspaper publishing business of a Spanish exile, Víctor Pey, a trusted member of the Allende circle, which had been expropriated by the Pinochet regime.

In 1991 Spain signed a treaty with the new civilian government of Chile establishing reciprocal guarantees on investment and the duty of each side to compensate the other for any violations of the agreement. The unwillingness of Chile to compensate Pey and the Fundación Salvador Allende with which he was associated for the losses suffered under Pinochet allowed the matter to be put to the International Centre for the Settlement of Investment Disputes in April 1998.

The case is still being argued at the time of writing. If the case is resolved in the Fundación Salvador Allende's favour and payment of suitable compensation is made it could be a significant precedent in the fight to have the arbitrary actions of those such as Pinochet punished.

Friends in the Vatican

Over the years Pinochet put much energy into improving relations with the Catholic Church from the low point to which they had sunk during the times of Raúl Silva. The wisdom of his policy was now revealed. He retained many friends at the pontifical court, a factor which was to produce dividends for him in the late 1990s.

Chilean-born Cardinal Jorge Medina was a long-standing friend; the conservative Colombian Cardinal Alfonso López Trujillo inclined towards him; he seemed to have the ear of Cardinal Joseph Ratzinger, and also that of the present Archbishop Francisco Javier

Errázuriz of Santiago, a member of the conservative Schönstatt group within the Catholic Church, who had held high posts in the Vatican before his appointment.

In February 1999, Cardinal Sodano let it be known that he had intervened the previous November on the General's behalf with the British Government and with the Archbishop of Canterbury. Cardinal Sodano's intervention, according to Mgr Piero Pioppo, secretary at the nunciature in Santiago, was the result of an appeal from the Chilean government to the Holy See that Chile's sovereignty in the matter of Pinochet should be respected. Throughout his reign Pope John Paul II had been a strong supporter of national sovereignty. This was particularly true for his native country, Poland, although his very public reprimands for Catholics who supported the Sandinista government in Nicaragua against the Contra terrorists made it clear that he would offer no support to the Nicaraguan government's struggle against US aggression in Central America.

The Chilean political scene was thrown into confusion by Sodano's appeal. For his part, President Eduardo Frei Ruiz-Tagle had pushed for Pinochet to escape trial in Spain. But even Christian Democrats, whose party is the largest in the centre-left coalition which, under quiet military tutelage, governs Chile and opposes General Pinochet's extradition to Spain, had expressed their opposition to the Vatican move. Gabriel Asencio, a Christian Democratic deputy, argued, 'With all the respect that in my opinion the church merits, I would never have accepted its intervention in favour of Hitler. They have no right to intervene when what is at stake here is a matter of universal justice.'

After the General had been in confinement for nine months he acquired an unexpected ally in his fight to be returned to Chile. At the June 1999 summit of leaders of the European Union and Latin America held in Rio de Janeiro, President Fidel Castro of Cuba – with whom Pinochet had been locked in a battle of mutual antipathy for more than a quarter of a century – issued a call for him to be released from custody in England. The national sensibilities of Latin America, he explained, demanded nothing less. Equally surprisingly Felipe González also called for his return to Chile, a statement which caused much anger in the Spanish Socialist Party.

Footing the bill

'You can't put a cost to the people who have been tortured or
disappeared',
Andy McEntee, chairman Amnesty International,
British section.

After Pinochet's arrest on charges of genocide, terrorism, murder,
illegal detention, kidnapping and torture, the course of British law
wound slowly on. Many observers of the process were surprised at
the almost incomprehensible legal traditions and practices: the wigs,
the bowing, the strange titles. Such traditions and practices were
often the result of a deliberated, centuries-old process of obfuscation
and to most outside Britain they must have seemed unfathomable.

Directly after the news of the arrest was announced a small anti-
Pinochet crowd descended on the London Clinic and were to stay
there for days, kept in check by the Metropolitan Police. Their
cries and jeers certainly reached Pinochet, whose room faced onto
the road where his opponents had gathered. They also reached and
disturbed the Clinic's other patients and it soon became clear that
the hospital's management wanted to move on their notorious
patient as soon as possible.

Under police guard, Pinochet was moved to another hospital in
the north-western suburbs of London. When he was released he
settled in a sparsely-furnished house on the Wentworth Estate some
25 kms south-west of the centre of the capital. This served as home
for him and the police who kept custody of the General round the
clock.

His lawyers were quick to move against his detention. Setting
aside the question of whether he was or was not guilty of the crimes
with which he was charged, they held that as a former head of state
he enjoyed immunity from prosecution in Britain. In a hearing on
25-28 October they asked for Pinochet's release on the grounds
that his detention was unlawful.

The Crown Prosecution Service, arguing for his extradition to
Spain on behalf of the Spanish state, opposed them. In front of
the Lord Chief Justice, Lord Bingham and two other senior judges,
Pinochet's lawyers won the hearing. The court, which sat with him

in the Victorian Gothic splendour of the Royal Courts of Justice, accepted Pinochet's defence that his actions had been those of a head of state and therefore, under the doctrine of sovereign immunity, could not be challenged.

However, in the closing minutes of the hearing, just as onlookers decided that one of the most sensational arrests of the century was over, the Lord Chief Justice gave the CPS leave to appeal to the House of Lords, the highest court in the land. He commented nevertheless that he thought they had small chance of winning there.

On 25 November, Pinochet's 83rd birthday, the Law Lords gave their verdict. They overturned the opinion of the Lord Chief Justice. Five of a small group of senior judges appointed to the House of Lords to serve on that chamber's judiciary committee and deliver judgement on the weightiest of legal matters decided by three votes to two that Pinochet did not have immunity from extradition. The crowd of his opponents who had congregated outside the Houses of Parliament danced and sang as the verdict was transmitted to them on their transistor radios.

The way was now clear for Jack Straw, the Home Secretary – who had not exercised his power to halt Pinochet's initial arrest on 17 October – to allow the extradition case to go ahead. The magistrate, Graham Parkinson, was given the job of considering for the first time the merits of the Spanish request for extradition. On 11 December, Pinochet, brought by a convoy of cars from his rented house, made his first public appearance in the special high security Belmarsh magistrates court in the south-east of the capital.

There he identified himself but refused to acknowledge the authority of the court over him. Parkinson, as was expected at what was only the formal beginning of a long and complicated case which Pinochet would not be required to attend in person, adjourned the case till 18 January. (In court Pinochet sat in a wheelchair, a vehicle he did not normally use. The impression he gave was of a person of some physical frailty and this corresponded to the campaign that his supporters had mounted for release of an invalid old man who deserved to be sent home on humanitarian grounds.)

In Madrid Garzón published nearly 400 pages containing charges of genocide, torture and terrorism against Pinochet. In London, on 14 December, Pinochet's defence team announced that they were impugning the House of Lords decision. Their grounds were that the South African-born Lord Hoffman, one of the five who had delivered the 25 November judgement, had been active on behalf of Amnesty International. The human rights group had submitted arguments to the Law Lords on the case and therefore he could not be considered to be impartial. Three days later, in an unprecedented decision to reconsider their previous verdict, a new group of Law Lords accepted the argument. The 25 November verdict was scrapped, a new hearing was to start on 18 January 1999.

In a world where cases often take years to be considered, the judges, conscious of the immense international interest, moved with speed. Disappointed though the anti-Pinochet side was, the new hearing was to prove a blessing in disguise. It allowed the world's experts on international law to make new submissions without haste.

Amid a fever of anticipation, a new judgement was delivered on March 25. Moved by the new evidence and the precedents which had been gathered and presented to them, the seven judges, presided over by Lord Browne-Wilkinson, found by six to one that Pinochet did not enjoy immunity. On the other hand they added that on the question of his extradition only charges relating to crimes alleged to have been committed after 29 September 1988 should be taken into account. That had been the date when international conventions against torture came into effect in British law. It eliminated much of what Garzón had accused him of in December. The written judgement, containing as it does the most searching analysis of the rights and restrictions of heads of state, will certainly go down as a weighty precedent in future cases of this nature.

Lord Browne-Wilkinson and his colleagues invited Jack Straw to reconsider his decision to allow extradition proceedings to continue. Amnesty International argued that torture was an international crime and a court of justice should be allowed to determine whether Augusto Pinochet is guilty or innocent of this crime. It dismissed the argument put forth by Pinochet's lawyers that given the reduction in the number of charges resulting from the House of Lords ruling, he could not be held responsible for acts of torture committed for most of the time he had been head of state, from 1973 to 1988. It was not true, said Amnesty, that the smaller the number of charges of torture for which he could be prosecuted made the case no longer fit for extradition.

'Arguments related to the reduction of charges should be dismissed as contrary to the word and spirit of the UN Convention Against Torture and to the House of Lords ruling,' it said. 'According to the Convention Against Torture, even one case of torture would be sufficient to permit extradition to a state able and willing to try the person accused,' the organisation continued. 'This will be the only way to give a chance to justice, to prove that international law goes beyond the signing of treaties and to offer to victims and relatives of human rights violations in Chile an opportunity to have their claim answered after 25 years of waiting.'

Amnesty added that his victims include 1,198 '"disappeared" people and their families, who have been subjected to a form of torture that will continue until the fate of the "disappeared" is re-solved.' International law has long established that forced disap-pearances on a widespread or systematic basis were crimes against humanity. 'All states have the obligation to exercise universal juris-diction to prosecute these crimes,' it stressed.

Jack Straw did review the situation. Finally, on 15 April, he decided that there were insufficient grounds to halt the consideration of extradition. Pinochet was again at risk.

The stage was set for another extradition hearing on 27 September. It started at the Bow Street magistrates court before Ronald Bartle, the deputy chief metropolitan stipendiary magistrate, with the Crown Prosecution Service, as before, representing Spain and presenting arguments for the extradition.

The days immediately before Bartle's decision were taken up by an extraordinary secret last-minute manoeuvre by the conservative government of Spanish Prime Minister José María Aznar. The government had been worried that protests by a pro-Pinochet Chilean establishment, resentful of Spain's bid to bring Pinochet to justice, could harm Spanish business interests in Chile and had quietly resisted Garzón's bid for his extradition insofar as it was able. It sent two officials, Miguel Aguirre de Cárcer, a foreign office offical, and Carmen de la Peña, legal officer at the embassy in London, to Brian Gibbens at the London offices of the Crown Prosecution Sevice. The diplomats' verbal message was that in the event of Bartle giving a judgement against Pinochet, the government of Spain would not necessarily lodge an appeal and that therefore the CPS should not do so without instructions from Madrid. The effect of any delay to an appeal would have been to allow Pinochet to be freed immediately and to return to Chile.

The import of the message was understood by Gibbens, who immediately sought clarification from the Spanish judicial authorities. Was there to be an immediate appeal against any pro-Pinochet judgement by Bartle, as Garzón had indicated, or was the CPS to suspend its activity as the diplomats had asked? Garzón himself was in Paraguay but he immediately arranged for a fellow judge to reiterate instructions to the CPS that they should lodge an immediate appeal and thus prevent Pinochet being freed and escaping on the next flight to Chile. The Aznar government was stymied and embarrassed. It initially denied the diplomats had approached the CPS, then pretended that they had not been speaking for the govenrment. The publication of Gibbens' letter seeking clarification completed Aznar's confusion. The Madrid daily *El País* rubbed the prime minister's nose in the dirt by calling the manoeuvre 'double-speak, cowardice and dirty tricks'.

On 8 October, Bartle, having excused Pinochet on grounds of ill-health from appearing personally, announced his decision that Pinochet's extradition to Spain would be legitimate.

By a decision of the Law Lords delivered at the beginning of July 1999, the British taxpayer was left with a bill of some £4 million to cover legal costs incurred by Pinochet. In December these costs had been estimated at £12,000 a day – in part due to the high charges of his two UK lawyers. Clive Nicholls QC was reported by *The Independent* newspaper to be charging £500 an hour and Clare Montgomery QC, £350 an hour. Junior barristers, of whom two or three would always be on hand, were charging about half that hourly fee. In addition the bill from the London firm of Kingsley Napley for the work undertaken by ten solicitors – lawyers working in the back rooms and not usually allowed to present arguments in court in major trials – was put at £4,500 a day.

Under the European Convention on Extradition the costs of the Crown Prosecution Service, which was acting on behalf of the Kingdom of Spain at the instance of Garzón, were borne by the British and not the Spanish government. Losing no opportunity to lambaste Jack Straw, the Home Secretary, Lord Lamont, the former British finance minister, declared, 'This expensive political farce should have been killed off long ago.'

Meanwhile Pinochet bore up as best he could in his mansion in Virginia Water with what he might call fortitude and Christian resignation. For their part his followers, a diminishing but still vocal group in Chile and Britain, could take comfort from the comment of his to a Chilean newspaper only a week after his arrest: 'In this world they also betrayed Christ'.

A brief chronology

1915	Augusto Pinochet born in Valparaiso, the eldest of three boys and three girls, 25 November
1933	Joins Military School
1937	Graduates as ensign, joins School of Infantry at San Bernardo Transferred to the Chacabuco Regiment, Concepción
1939	Transferred as Second Lieutenant to the Maipo Regiment in Valparaiso
1940	Returns to the School of Infantry
1940	Promoted First Lieutenant and posted to the Military School
1943	Marries Lucía Hiriart. Birth of Lucía, the first of three daughters and two sons
1945	Posted to the Carampangue Regiment in Iquique
1948	Passes entrance examination to the War Academy but entry delayed. Posted to Lota coal mines near Concepción
1949	Enters Academy
1951	Reaches staff officer rank, posted to Military School
1953	Promoted Major, posted to the Rancagua Regiment in Arica then to Academy of War
1956	Joins mission to Ecuador to establish War College in Quito
1959	Posted to the staff of the First Division in Antofagasta
1960	Appointed Commanding officer of the Esmeralda Regiment
1963	Appointed Deputy Director Academy of War
1968	Appointed Chief of Staff of the Second Division, promoted Brigadier-General, promoted to command the Sixth Division, in Iquique, appointed deputy governor of the Province of Tarapacá by the Christian Democrat government of President Eduardo Frei Montalva.
1971	Promoted to Major-General and appointed by President Salvador Allende to commander of the Santiago garrison
1972	Appointed Chief of the General Staff by President Allende
1973	Appointed Commander-in-Chief of the army (23 August), joins plot against Allende (8 September), seizes command of plot (11 September), sets up National Stadium in Santiago as a temporary prison, holding, according to Red Cross estimates, some 7,000 prisoners. Other concentration camps established at Pisagua, Chacabuco and Dawson Island remotely sited in the Straits of Magellan (12 September). DINA starts operating.
1974	Chile's electoral registers are declared invalid and burned.

Decree 527 vests all executive powers in the President of the Junta, General Augusto Pinochet (14 June). General Carlos Prats, Pinochet's predecessor as Army Commander-in-Chief is killed in Buenos Aires by a car bomb. His wife dies with him (30 September). (In April 1998 Argentine courts hold the Chilean secret police, DINA, responsible).

1975   Milton Friedman, founder of the Chicago School of Economics, visits Chile and is favourably impressed. Leading Christian Democrat and former deputy Bernardo Leighton and his wife are shot and seriously injured in Rome. DINA is held responsible (16 October).

1976   Spanish economist Carmelo Soria, on the staff of the United Nations and the holder of a UN diplomatic passport, found dead two days after disappearing in Santiago. DINA, the secret police, held responsible (16 July). Orlando Letelier, Allende's former Ambassador to the United States, is murdered by a car bomb in Washington DC, along with his American assistant Ronni Moffitt. DINA held responsible (21 September).

1977   DINA is replaced by the National Information Centre (CNI) which continues the same functions.

1978   State of Siege, in force since the coup, is suspended. Amnesty Law promulgated to pardon all individuals who committed crimes during the period of the State of Siege, 11 September 1973 to 10 March 1978 (19 April).

1980   A rigged plebiscite approves Pinochet's new constitution which makes Pinochet President for eight years after which a 'protected democracy' will be created; Andrés Zaldívar, President of the Christian Democrat Party, expelled from Chile for denouncing the new constitution as illegal.

1984   Regime issues a list of 5,000 Chileans prohibited from returning to their country.

1986   Carmen Gloria Quintana and Rodrigo Rojas arrested by a military patrol during protests in Santiago, doused in kerosene and set on fire by soldiers. Rojas dies, but Quintana survives with 60% burns. Pinochet escapes assassination attempt in Cañón del Maipu. Pinochet proclaims new state of siege. Various publications closed down and opposition leaders arrested.

1987   Pope John Paul II visits Chile.

1988   Pinochet loses plebiscite.

1989   Voters approve reforms to the 1980 constitution, paving the way for transition to a civilian government, but falling short of creating a full democracy. Pinochet is obliged to call elections, won by Patricio Aylwin.

1990　　Hands over presidency to Aylwin, retaining command of the army. Supreme Court upholds the 1978 Amnesty Law, thus precluding prosecutions for pre-1978 human rights violations. Pinochet confines troops to barracks and threatens violence to deter the government from investigating his son on fraud charges, and to warn President Aylwin against 'interfering' in the promotion of senior officers (19 December).

1991　　The Rettig Commission presents its report, concluding that at least 2,025 persons were killed or disappeared during the period of military rule (4 March).

1993　　Armed soldiers in camouflage uniform appear near the Moneda Palace while President Aylwin is out of the country, apparently as a warning against proceeding with human rights trials against army officers and any further investigation of his son Augusto.

Christian Democrat candidate Eduardo Frei Ruiz-Tagle elected President to replace Aylwin (11 December).

1997　　A bill to eliminate the designated senators established in the 1980 Constitution fails in Congress.

1998

10 March　　Pinochet hands command of the army to General Ricardo Izurieta.

11 March　　Sworn in as Life Senator amid riots in Valparaiso.

21 September　Pinochet flies to London to visit UK arms suppliers and Lady Thatcher.

22 September　Pinochet arrives in London.

8 October　　Pinochet enters London Clinic for operation on spinal hernia.

16 October　　Warrant served on Pinochet at the London Clinic by Scotland Yard for extradition to face charges of crimes against humanity.

28 October　　High Court grants Pinochet immunity as former head of state.

November　　On behalf of the Kingdom of Spain, the Crown Prosecution Service appeals successfully against High Court ruling.

25 November　Law Lords rule by 3-2 majority that Pinochet's status as former head of state does not give him immunity.

9 December　　The Home Secretary, Jack Straw, authorises extradition proceedings.

22 December	After an appeal by Pinochet's lawyers, the Law Lords set aside their initial ruling because of Lord Hoffmann's links to Amnesty International.

1999

24 March	The Law Lords rule 6-1 that Pinochet may be extradited on the basis of crimes against humanity committed after 8 December 1988 when Britain and Chile ratified the International Torture Convention.
14 April	Jack Straw, the Home Secretary, decides to authorise extradition proceedings.
27 September	An extradition procedure started at the Bow Street magistrates court. The Crown Prosecution Service representing Spain airis evidence of torture and conspiracy to torture.
8 October	Ronald Bartle, chief deputy metropolitan stipendiary magistrate, having excused Pinochet on grounds of ill-health from appearing personally, announced his decision that Pinochet's extradition to Spain would be legitimate.

Bibliography

A good introduction to Chile is found in Nick Caistor's *Chile* in the Latin America Bureau's In Focus series (London, 1999) and there is no better travel guide to Chile than that contained in the annual *South American Handbook*, edited by Ben Box.

The best sources on the life and times of Augusto Pinochet are obviously to be found in Spanish. The work published under his own name, especially the four-volume *Camino Recorrido, Memorias de un Soldado*, (Instituto Geográfico Militar, Santiago 1990-1998) set out his life as he would like it to be viewed. The immediate circumstances of the coup are thrillingly described by Patricia Verdugo in *Interferencia Secreta; 11 de septiembre de 1973*, (Editorial Sudamericana, Santiago, 1998), complete with a CD of the conversations as recorded from the plotters' various command posts.

Chile's Road to Socialism (Penguin, London, 1973) is a useful compendium of Allende's thought expressed in his own words. In *Revolutionary Social Democracy : The Chilean Socialist Party*, (Frances Pinter, London 1986) Benny Pollack and Hernán Rosenkranz give a sound analysis of the Chilean left.

Ian Roxborough, Philip O'Brien and Jackie Roddick's *Chile, the State and Revolution* (Macmillan, London, 1977) and Robinson Rojas Sandford's *The Murder of Allende* and *The Chilean Way to Socialism* (Harper and Row, New York, 1975) are useful views of the Allende years.

La Historia Oculta del Régimen Militar by Ascanio Cavallo, Manuel Salazar and Oscar Sepúlveda and its companion volume *La Historia Oculta de la Transición* by Ascanio Cavallo (Grijalbo, Santiago, 1997-8) are serious vivid and revealing.

Cardinal Silva wrote three volume of memoirs with Cavallo (Ediciones Copygraph, Santiago 1991) which understandably concentrate on church matters.

Allende et l'Expérience chilienne by Juan Garcés and a further volume *Orlando Letelier, Testimonio y vindicación*, which Garcés wrote in collaboration with Saul Landau, are authoritative studies of the Allende government and the assassination of Allende's foreign and defence minister.

John Dinges and Landau also wrote the excellent *Assassination on Embassy Row*.

For information on chemical weapons refer to *Labyrinth* (Penguin Books, London, 1983) by Taylor Branch and Eugene M. Propper.

The Valkyrie Operation (Blake Publishing, London, 1998) by Wensley Clarkson gives a vivid account of Jonathan Moyle's life.

Tomás Moulián has been among the commentators about Chile during the presidencies of Aylwin and Frei Ruiz-Tagle. Among his best books is *Chile Actual: Anatomía de un Mito* (Arcis, Santiago, 1997)

The author contributed to a volume of essays, *Chile: Tragedia Americana* (Editorial Crisis, Buenos Aires, 1974).

Index